Boxing

THE GREAT ONES

Boxing
THE GREAT ONES

Reg Gutteridge

PELHAM BOOKS

First published in Great Britain by Pelham Books Ltd
52 Bedford Square, London WC1
1975

© 1975 by Reg Gutteridge

ISBN 0 7207 0592 4

Set and printed in Great Britain by
Tonbridge Printers Ltd, Peach Hall Works,
Tonbridge, Kent, in Baskerville eleven on
thirteen point on paper supplied by
P. F. Bingham Ltd, and bound by
James Burn at Esher, Surrey

Contents

Eight pages of illustrations
are between pages 80 and 81

Introduction

Boxing – The Great Ones, a rather dubious title! I can hear the arguments raging already, 'Who does this Gutteridge chap think he is, selecting nine boxers from the history of the game, and calling them the great ones!'

Before anyone starts taking legal action against me I think I should point out that these nine boxers are a *selection* of the greats of all time. I could quite easily name thirty or forty boxers who deserve the title great one. But a book of that size would be impractical and I had to trim the numbers down. From that initial list of thirty or forty I selected the men in this book. I selected them because *I* found them the most interesting and entertaining, because *I* enjoyed watching them in action either 'live' or on film.

Within the book there has been no selection of position at all. The fact that Ali appears first and Jimmy Wilde last does not mean that I think that Ali is the greatest ever and Wilde the ninth greatest, they just happen to fall that way.

Anyway, see what you think, whatever you say, these are some of the great names of the business!

I
Muhammad Ali

If I could have handpicked a sportsman, any sportsman, of any era, and have to report his life and times, it would be Muhammad Ali. I have covered the majority of his fights and, on two occasions, in Switzerland and Indonesia, was the only British writer at ringside.

Fifteen years of watching, praising, criticising and often gasping at Ali's antics have been rewarding. I have been a backstage confidante, an observer of Ali's incredible lifestyle, a fellow passenger on tiresome flights and I have even been considered as part of his entourage.

The man who became the best-known face in the world continues to confuse. Ali is the godsend to the media, a man who spoils newseekers and photographers. He never says No.

For example, ringside reports of Ali from America and Zaire added almost 100,000 additional sales to the London *Evening News*, with editions published at 9.30 a.m. Ali is, unquestionably, the most news-worthy figure of our time. TV recordings of his fights, when the result is known, have regularly reached the top three of the viewer ratings. He is the most widely publicised, and most controversial, sportsman of all time. He is an amazingly contradictory character. He can be both aloof and friendly; he is rarely openly rude to whites and yet he publicly preaches the Elijah Muhammad Black Muslim view that all whites are devils.

Ali, who officially adopted the religion at Miami Beach a few hours after becoming world heavyweight champion in

1964, is the sect's most devout disciple. Whether or not the Muslims who move in Ali's circle are equally devoted to the cause is a matter of opinion. I have no right, nor desire, to tangle with Ali or his associates about their beliefs of race separatism.

Debating with Ali, as BBC interviewer, Michael Parkinson discovered, is a lost cause because Ali disbelieves argument that has not been taught him by his Chicago leader, Elijah. Elijah's son, Herbert, a polite and unobtrusive man, officially manages and dominates Ali.

I have told Ali that if I agreed with many of the Muslim teachings and if he wanted to prove that the sect was not, as he often claims, restricted to black muslims why could I not enrol? He regards counter questioning as 'trick baiting'. 'Your heart's in the right place' he says 'And that's sufficient'.

You can't win with Ali. He can change from a whispering, seemingly bored person to an irrational, angry zealot. But he has never, in my experience, been seen to be violent outside of business hours. He can be overwhelmingly generous, even to strangers, and his devotion to children, of all creeds, is genuine.

He is not a person easily engaged in small-talk unless you are accepted by him. He does not freely offer handshakes. He can switch on and off without warning. He will sign autographs for hours without complaining but detests being manhandled. He has thrown a punch at his aide, Drew (Bundini) Brown, for trying to hug him after a second tremendous fight against Ken Norton.

His religous/racial hobby horse rantings are for real. His 'I'm the greatest' shouting and the taunting of past or prospective opponents is phoney. He began the outrageous egotism technique after watching an all-in wrestler, the late Gorgeous George, irritate his audience.

Tricking and putting-on is a natural desire and a sense of fun for Ali. There is a lot of boy in the man and he should not be hated for the pose of arrogance. He is encouraged by promoters – and the media. I have heard frustrated publicity pedlars plead with Ali for more action to help them sell seats.

Hopefully, I have gained Ali's respect, if not his friendship, because I have maintained a professional detachment and refused to be among his fawning set.

Yet, no matter how contradictory or controversial Ali might be, my admiration for him as a boxer and entertainer remains unimpaired by his current desire to be an avenging racial angel.

Until Ali regained the richest prize in sport in 1974 I was not totally convinced that he is the greatest heavyweight of all. Joe Louis held sway. Jack Johnson was also a master. Others would argue the case for deadly hitters Jack Dempsey and Rocky Marciano.

But Ali has brought a new conception to the art of boxing. It took a long time to accept his way-out style. He is not the hardest of heavyweight hitters and his in-fighting is practically non-existent. Ali's greatness, apart from the grace, the speed and the beautiful art of swaying out of harm's way, is more basic. He *takes* a blow better than anyone else. Behind the show off is a brave heart and a body that has recuperative powers beyond all other big men.

He was also the first to bring pure athleticism to heavyweight boxing. It is a myth that Ali is a natural athlete because he has never been better than average and certainly never excelled at any other sport. But there was an indescribable grace about the peak Ali at work. He likes only to be compared to being a larger edition of Sugar Ray Robinson. Ali will be regarded by historians as 'a natural' but, in fact, he worked at developing the style. Ali is a boxing lover despite his occasional dismissal of a game that brought him fame and presented him with a stage to cock a snoot at American society.

Of the past nine heavyweight champions, eight have been black. Ali, however, was the first to proclaim his blackness and to say to the white world 'I don't have to be what you want me to be'. He is the first black champion in history not to have been the puppet of white promoters. The man who became a Belafonte with boxing gloves is the ideal practitioner to preach the message that *Black is Beautiful.*

He is not only faster but bigger than his predecessors. Aside from Primo Carnera and Jess Willard, who were freaks, Ali is the most sizeable of all. He was outweighed by George Foreman, who turned out to be bully who buckled under fire, but his physical attributes were generally superior.

Ali is supreme in an age of giant men. It is impossible to imagine blown up light-heavyweights like Dempsey and Marciano, who weighed less than $13\frac{1}{2}$ st., being able to defeat Ali. At peak Ali's best was 15 st. 4 lb. though he was 15 st. when he first won the title.

Louis the magnificent who, perhaps, landed his blows closer to text book teachings than Ali, was knocked down eight times in his 17 pro years. He was beaten three times – twice by knockout at the peak and fag end of his career.

In 47 fights, a record truncated by an enforced three year lay off, Ali has not been stopped or knocked out. Ali has been hit by super punchers – but has yet to stay hit. He came off the floor against Sonny Banks, Henry Cooper and Joe Frazier. His recovery against Cooper and Frazier, both potent left hookers, was phenomenal. He was adjudged the points loser in the first 15-rounds clash with Frazier yet Ali, who claimed that he had landed at least double the amount of blows, could arguably have won the fifteenth round after being knocked down by the blow of a lifetime.

Ali is only the second heavyweight to have regained the world crown. Floyd Patterson, the youngest to win the title at 21, was the first but Patterson (twice hammered by Ali) lost and won against the same opponent, Ingemar Johansson. Ali had not lost his crown in the ring and he won it twice against awesome punchers, Sonny Liston and George

Foreman. I was privileged to have reported both title fights. I must admit that twice I had picked the wrong guy! I believed Liston, a brutal hitter and bully, would prove too strong for a then excitable 22-year-old who fought under his birthname of Cassius (Marcellus) Clay. I wrote that Clay, the Kentucky Rooster, was destined for greatness – winning an Olympic gold medal at 18 was sufficient evidence – but feared that in 1964 he was fighting Liston too early in his career. It was against better judgment, believing head ruled heart, that I considered George Foreman, at 25, with 40 unbeaten fights (37 opponents failing to survive) might bludgeon an Ali who appeared to be on the wane at 32. Foreman had won his previous eight contests, including blasting Frazier and Ken Norton who had both outpointed Ali, within two rounds. Foreman had a capacity for obliteration but faced by a fearless Ali he turned out to be a mere fighting Frankenstein. His brain and body could not cope with the shocks inflicted.

The Ali-Foreman battle took place in Africa at 4 a.m. on October 31, 1974. It was a present to the people of the independent state of Zaire (formerly Belgian Congo) from the president Mobutu Sese Seko. It was spectacular and expensive.

The president had hired Ali, the greatest salesman in history, to project Zaire. The promotion lost money. Ali and Foreman both had pre-fight banked purses of five million dollars (roughly two and a half million pounds) and a two months postponement, due to Foreman's eyebrow being cut in sparring, was costly.

Overpricing at closed-circuit TV venues in America and Britain, plus a spate of publicity that doubted if the fight would ever take place reduced the total take. The consortium of Hemdale in London, Video Techniques in New York and the Zaire government, had over-estimated the returns for their first fight venture. The Viewsport company closed-circuit takings in Britain were the highest ever – but they did not make a profit after paying £300,000-plus for the TV rights.

It proves that anyone can be a fight promoter if they put up the money. But not anyone can make a profit. The only sure winners were Ali and Foreman, though the way Foreman forfeited his crown devalued his future earnings.

It was not the most thrilling fight I have seen, but it was the most bizarre. The atmosphere, the expectancy, the excitement at ringside was not captured by TV screens on other continents.

The total supremacy of Ali the underdog, the hero of the Africans, provided the story of the decade. His eighth round knockout, was delivered with the coupe de grace of a matador who had skilfully tired a bull.

Like Manolete, Ali possessed the gift of escaping the bull's charges by a fraction. But Ali did not require his customary grace against Foreman. Ali's tactics had confused Foreman, his own cornermen and the critics. We had expected the rehearsed Ali dance and shuffle, swivelling as though wearing roller skates, in the plan to wear Foreman down. Instead, Foreman became a victim of his own conceit that brawn would beat brain. It was an Ali example of mind over matter. Ali pysched and punched all the fight out of Foreman by talking and taunting 'This is the wrong place to get tired'. Ali propped himself against the ropes deliberately offering his body for Foreman to hit.

For minutes on end Foreman clubbed at Ali's body, but rarely reached his face, while Ali waited for the 15 st. 10 lb. champion to burn himself out. It seemed an admirable yet foolish trait that would affect Ali's proficiency. Who but Ali would sacrifice his body against a known big hitter?

Ali's strength was in his tactics. He broke Foreman's spirit before wrecking his body. Ali continued to taunt Foreman 'Is that the best you can do?' and 'O.K. sucker, now it's my turn'.

The chilling confidence we had seen from Foreman in

previous fights melted in the 90 per cent humidity of the 20th May soccer stadium in Kinshasa (formerly Leopoldville). Foreman grunted like an angry rhino trying to beat his way out of a bush. He played into Ali's hands by not varying his tactics. Foreman's movements were mechanical. I was surprised that Foreman's cornermen, Sandy Saddler and Archie Moore, both the greatest of ex-champions, were unable to influence him. But as Moore confided afterwards: 'George fought that way because Ali made him fight that way. I have to concede now that Ali must be the greatest.' Old Archie, however, did not concede total defeat by adding 'Muhammad was once a protégé of mine, you know'. Moore was also a victim of Ali – but the once master of the light-heavies was past his prime when a rising Cassius Clay knocked him out, as predicted, in round four.

Zach Clayton, one-time Harlem globetrotter who refereed the fight in Zaire, permitted too much wrestling. He rarely called 'break' but forcibly pulled the heavies apart as the sprays of sweat bounced off their bodies.

Oxygen containers were propped in both corners but were unused.

The contest was surely the first title offering in history not to be announced from the ring. The champion and challenger entered, stood for the national anthems, and then got on with it. We should have known from the off that Ali had lifted himself for his greatest hour. He had drawn strength from being in Africa for eight weeks, though he is essentially a black American and does not fully understand African history. (Ali was affronted by a Nigerian journalist who rightly pointed out that it was African chiefs who originally sold their tribes to white slavers. Where was the brotherhood in that? 'My leader don't never teach me nuthin like that' Ali answered.) Ali had looked down at us at the commentators bench, sorting out David Frost who was broadcasting with Bob Sheridan to American closed-circuit, and feigned fear as he looked at Foreman. He trembled his hands, knocked his knees and then laughed. 'I'll get your ass' I heard him spit through his gumshield to Foreman.

The champion, who had kept Ali waiting, and then jogged across the soccer pitch to the ring, sweated profusely.

Ali had preached that his now veteran style of standing his ground and adding weight to his punches would finish Foreman. And he was right. Foreman's legs began to un-hinge after the sixth round. His muscular mass, as often happens, became a disadvantage. It was as though Foreman had been struck by athletic senility. He had punched himself out and the flurries of punches that Ali landed had swiftly weakened him.

Foreman made a stronger effort in the eighth and, for almost a minute, looked as if he could turn the tide of battle. Ali was biding his time, but that was hard to judge. Commentator Harry Carpenter, who has seen Ali in action more than most, noted 'Ali can hardly hold his hands up'. But the hands came up at the right time to catch Foreman off balance and unguarded. Two right clips on the point of the jaw spun Foreman around as he pitched face downwards for the first count and first knockout of his career. Foreman could not cope with the indignity, pain and confusion of being put down.

Foreman's fall shook the ring. His eyes were like marbles and though he had lifted himself to his haunches by the time the count reached ten the referee was right to declare Foreman 'out' in the act of rising.

Foreman, inevitably, complained that the count was fast and that he was up at the stroke of nine. He also beefed about the loosening of ropes during the contest. Neither complaint had any validity.

Ali's long-time second, Angelo Dundee, had instructed aides to tighten not loosen ropes because he feared Ali would fall out of the four-roped ring. The top rope sagged under the continued weight of the big men being draped over it like wet laundry.

Ali had led the crowd in war chants of 'Bom-aye-yeah (Kill Him) between the rounds, had offered his Muslim prayer in the corner, and was upset when knocked over by a posse of white-helmeted police who stormed the ring after the fight.

When the protectors finally led a jubilant Ali and entourage back to the dressing rooms we worried about wiring our words in a hurry back to London. Fortunately, the communications worked – but only just.

Within an hour of Ali's victory the heavens opened and torrential rain flooded the ringside area. The roads around the stadium turned to rivers as the storms raged. It was as though darkest Africa was paying its tribute to sport's finest sorcerer.

Ten years and eight months earlier Ali had shocked the majority of the fight world by pysching the powerful Sonny Liston. The Louisville Lip, with only nineteen pro fights, was pitted against a champion whose ears seemed to sprout muscles.

Only three of the 59 critics questioned in a snap poll around the ringside at Miami Beach on February 25, 1964, gave the then Cassius Clay a chance. My New York friend, Bob Waters, made a name for himself by predicting a k.o. win for the challenger (and he did likewise when Ali, again the underdog, obliged against Foreman).

Liston had a cruel remoteness to his cruel business and had twice annihilated Floyd Patterson, then reckoned to have the fastest hands in heavyweight history, in the first round.

Looking at Liston gave the impression that he would reign for ever. He weighed 15 st. 8 lb. Even Marciano, the fearless one, had told me that he would not have relished being in the same ring as Liston. Yet Ali, by confusing Liston with words and guile, reduced him to a fumbling automaton.

8,297 paid a then £1,785,000 at the air conditioned Miami

Convention Hall. Although Clay was locally trained and moulded at the Fifth Street gym owned by the Dundee brothers, he was 7–1 against winning. The odds did not look prohibitive except that Patterson had really been more of an accomplice than an opponent against Liston and had, no doubt, flattered Liston's punch power.

Willie Pastrano, who was world light-heavyweight champion and possessed immaculate skills, pleaded with me to tip Clay. But I was not then convinced that Clay had the ability and the experience to back up his boasts.

The weigh-in, normally a perfunctory and meaningless affair, was an embarrassment. We had never before witnessed such an exhibition of what turned out to be self-induced hysteria by Clay. He arrived wearing a denim jacket with 'Bear Huntin' written in red script. He thumped the floor with a heavy wooden cane and screamed himself hoarse yelling 'I'm ready to rumble, I'm the champ, you're a chump' and sweat showed on his face.

This was the first big act from Clay. It fooled even the shrewdest of observers. Colleague J. L. Manning reckoned Clay was in a state of nervous hysteria and the fight should be called off. Dr Alexander Robbins, of the Miami Boxing Commission, said 'Clay is nervous and scared and he's burning up a lot of energy'. When Clay refused to abandon his screaming (handlers pretended to restrain him from throwing punches at the astounded Liston), the chairman of the boxing commission, Morris Klein, stepped up to the microphone and announced 'Clay is fined 2,500 dollars for misconduct'.

As challenger Clay was collecting a then chicken feed 600,000 dollars. Liston earned one and a half million. Sugar Ray Robinson who was standing alongside Clay on stage looked distinctly embarrassed. But Angelo Dundee knew that Clay was purposely pysching Liston, a man who struck so much fear into others. 'Liston was so shook up he couldn't talk. He just didn't know what to make of the kid,' said Dundee.

Dr Pacheco, of Miami, who was to become Clay's totally unpaid aide, recalls that when Clay switched off his insulting act his pulse rate was normal. Yet Dr Robbins had insisted that Clay was 'liable to crack up, he's emotionally unbalanced'.

This was the fight when the now famous 'Float like a butterfly, sting like a bee' slogan was invented by Bundini Brown and chorused by Clay.

The fight produced a series of inexplicable happenings. Clay had showed fierce contempt as though he had knowledge that Liston's poleaxing fists were paralysed. Liston's left cheek was swollen and bleeding, this confounded the back-of-the-hall cynics who thought Clay was not hurting him.

Liston was reduced to mediocrity by the bemusing speed of his challenger. He was enraged enough to charge at Clay and fierce exchanges were shared. After six rounds the referee, Barney Felix, was scoring the fight level; one judge was calling it four rounds to one in Clay's favour and the other made Liston ahead by three rounds to two.

But the mixed scoring was only half the fun. In the fifth round Ali had wanted to quit when complaining that he was being blinded by a substance either on Liston's gloves or his hair. He reduced the round to slow motion. It seemed the medical opinion of Ali 'cracking up' may have been right. He behaved like a frightened child. When Clay returned to his corner he was roaring 'He's trying to blind me. He's got something on his gloves or head. I know by the way he's trying to charge at me.' But Dundee, a superb cornerman, yelled and forcibly shoved Clay back into the fray. The sixth was an incredible walking pace round with Clay lolling carelessly on the ropes, patting Liston's head, as though he were inviting Liston to put an end to his fears of being blinded. Clay was, in fact, stalling for time but he never suspected that he was only three minutes away from becoming world champion.

Liston bludgeoned and aimed sufficient punches to knock

out lesser men than Clay, but before the end of the sixth Clay resumed normal service after his inoffensive charade. He forced Liston to back pedal for the first time in his life – and for his first defeat in ten years.

Liston's pole of a left was being pushed out with a limber motion and there was still some obstinacy in his fighting. On my card Liston had won two rounds and had stunned Clay with some rib-bending blows. What we did not suspect was that Liston was apparently fighting through a coma of pain.

Sparing you the sanguinary details Liston's left shoulder was crocked with bursitis. He quit on the stool after the sixth round. Liston shook his head and seemed to lower it with shame while Clay leaped in disbelief as bedlam broke.

There were cries of 'Fix', there were boos and Liston was carted off to St Francis hospital where he stayed for three and a half hours. He came out with his arm in a sling, a tape over his cheek, and a baleful look.

Eight doctors examined 30-year-old Liston and a spokesman told us 'Liston's injury would be sufficient to incapacitate him and prevent him from defending himself.'

The medical terminology was 'an injury to the long head of the bicep tendon of the left shoulder with the result there is a separation and tear of muscle fibre with some hemorrhage of the muscle belly'. It was not, of course, a permanent disability.

I have known boxers to wage war and win with bigger physical handicaps during a contest, but Liston did not have the moral fibre. There is also a doubt that he was sufficiently well-trained to have lasted a longer distance. Liston had under-estimated Ali and shirked training. Perhaps he sensed that Clay had his measure and decided to get out of the fight at least with an acceptable excuse rather than be cut to ribbons and humiliated as Clay grew in stature.

One thing for certain; no man throws away a world championship.

It was, as I wrote at the time, the biggest upset since Sitting

Bull slaughtered Custer. Inevitably, my newspaper headlined 'The feat of Clay'.

It was not until Boxing Day, 1974, that Ali offered us some explanation of the 'blinding' incident of the fifth round. In an ITV World of Sport interview Ali revealed that a New York character 'I know who he is, but not his name. He's an Italian looking man' had suggested that Ali smear his gloves with a substance that would not blind an opponent but would cause pain.

'He said the stuff would burn the eyes and he wanted me to use it against George Foreman. I refused. That same man was hanging around the Liston corner in Miami. Now I'm sure that's what happened in that fight. I'm not saying Liston even knew about it, but somebody tried to harm me.'

I asked Ali if he had ever been propositioned to lose a fight? 'No, never' he replied.

There was the inevitable rematch with Liston, yet another blatant misuse of the pernicious return-clause contract. Maybe next time Liston would prove that he was the victim of a genuine and painful injury. Maybe he would also discipline his life – Liston was known for his heavy drinking between training stints – and report in fit and proper condition. The stigma of the Miami surrender had frightened off promoters and some State governors were even refusing permission for the replay championship to take place. Harold Conrad, a former newspaperman, Hollywood script writer, novelist, and publicity wizard, was the figure who finally persuaded the powers that the next fight would be the greatest of all time. Conrad's track record was useful. He had said similiar things when selling the two Patterson-Liston punch up's to the cities of Chicago and Las Vegas. Both finished in a couple of minutes.

Boston, Mass, displayed interest and, more importantly, put up the front money for Liston to prove that he could never be as bad a second time. With Clay having turned

Boxing: The Great Ones

Ali and spouting racial invectives the sourpuss Liston, ex-convict, was actually cast in the role of hero.

All was set for Boston to stage part two but only three days before the 'off' Ali was rushed to hospital for a hernia operation. Promoters scattered and the fight was in danger of being outlawed. Nobody wanted to touch it with a barge pole. But Conrad with the backing of a Philadelphia machine vendor, Sam Margolis, discovered a roller-rink shed in the unlikely hick town of Lewiston, Maine, and the State governor gave the go-ahead. It was the weirdest fight setting, with the smallest capacity, since Dempsey did his thing in Shelby, Montana.

The meeting took place on May 25, 1965. They built St Dominic's Arena at the foot of a descent once known as Skunk Hill: But nobody could have dreamed of a world title fight taking place there and causing such a stench.

Liston lasted an official sixty seconds, counted out without an actual count, in a time that was afterwards logged on TV as 2 min. 35 secs. He was also felled with a punch that was described from Phantom to karate, corkscrew to killer.

My ringside despatch carried the description 'an inconsequential slap' though I hasten to add that I would not invite Ali to hit me with a similar slap. Ali had timed his blow superbly, a right clip over a lumbering Liston left lead, and it was obviously sharp and surprising enough to stun Liston.

But since Ali had caught Britain's craggy faced hero heavyweight, Henry Cooper, with similar punches and failed to floor him, I could not fathom how a trained big man like Liston – whom Cooper had no desire to fight – should be grovelling on the canvas with his legs kicking like a moth caught in a flame.

There are endless excuses for Liston's inept defeat. The referee, Jersey Joe Walcott, a former heavyweight champion and honourable man, was wrong to allow Ali to be standing over Liston and calling 'Get up, ya Bum' while the ageing timekeeper was tolling a count that was barely audible.

Walcott (later to become mayor of Camden, New Jersey) should have abandoned the timekeeper's count until Ali obeyed his order to return to a neutral corner. Instead, Ali behaved like a dervish and Liston obviously had no intention of getting up until he could at least spot some light between him and his conqueror.

With Walcott wondering where to turn next, and Ali gesturing, Liston finally managed to haul himself up and even before Walcott could formally wave 'box on' Ali was raining further blows upon the confused (for the second time) Liston. But Walcott called a halt to the proceedings before Ali could nail Liston with a punch that looked more like a winner than his first twister, and before Liston could be given the chance to fight back. Nat Fleischer, the historian Mr Boxing, was waving for Walcott's attention. Fleischer, who should not have interfered, stood up to tell Walcott that the time-keeper, who was too weak to be heard, had counted Liston out.

With the heavyweights eyeing each other and Liston, perhaps, regaining his senses Walcott signalled that the fight – well, the affair – was over.

They had collected £3,833 each for every second of the event. The fight was the first event to be transmitted from America to Britain by Early Bird satellite.

Writer Jesse Abramson said he hoped that European fans watching the first satellite fight would have seen the punch 'for the sake of boxing's frayed integrity'. My colleague George Whiting wrote. 'It was a shambling apology for a world championship fight.' Peter Wilson came out swinging with 'It was a sickening, disgusting, revolting, utterly tasteless and nauseating travesty of an affair.'

I do not believe that Liston, in the parlance of the game, took a dive. His career was virtually finished that night. He was a mystery man, a one-time hoodlum surrounded by shady characters, and he died in mysterious circumstances a few years later.

I argued long and loud with Liston whom I did not consider to be quite the bad guy that he was cracked up to be. Liston said he would have got up if Ali had been pulled away. He also insisted that he was waiting to hear a count. Since Walcott never even indicated, let alone mouthed a count, there is some sympathy for Liston.

The finish was too ridiculous to have been a fix. There must have been more acceptable exit methods for Liston had he wanted to quit without being hurt. Liston was never forgiven for his fold-up, though time showed that another muscle man Foreman was put down and out with a punch that seemed only a fraction more solid than the flick of the Ali wrist that ruined Liston's fighting life. There must be a deceptive power behind those seemingly flicked punches.

The two Ali fights that generated the most tremendous excitement in this country were those against eleven-year British champion, Henry Cooper. Ali had the utmost respect for Cooper's left-hook that induced discomfort at short notice. He has also displayed the utmost courtesy to Cooper in his retirement years, though Ali's claims of showing compassion in both fights when Cooper's eyebrows was horribly gashed are not to be accepted without argument.

In fact, Ali did not withhold any punches, nor did he move them off the target of Cooper's injuries until the referee stepped in. Then Ali displayed compassion. He does not enjoy winning when he causes blood flow but he also talks glibly of his 'cutting punches'. This is yet another contradictory facet of Ali.

The first clash with Cooper, on the centre spot of Wembley's soccer pitch in 1963, was a non-title fight. It was intended to be Ali's warm-up on the way to challenge Liston. It almost turned out too hot for him. Cooper lost, as Ali had predicted, in five rounds. But the fight or, to be precise, one particular punch, made Henry famous and adored. Yes, Our 'Enery almost buttoned the Louisville Lip with a hook that dumped Ali down and had him looking like a rag doll with the stuffing coming out.

The fight had see-sawed evenly until round four and Cooper had not been overawed. He seemed able to take Ali's stiffest shots without flinching. There were moments when we suspected the Clay of the day of doing his 'carrying' act by half-hearted hitting. But Ali has conned the fans for a long time by play acting when, in fact, he is incapable of taking an opponent out. He tends to bide time, waiting with a hunter's patience for the kill, and the technique gives the impression of Ali deliberately holding back.

Ali moved away from Cooper in the fourth round with a lackadaisical look but he was not far enough out of range to permit himself that liberty. Cooper, the best one-punch hitter among Britain's long line of heavies, cracked a left-hook on Ali's jaw that dropped him like a log. Ali was propped against the ropes and appeared to be showing re-markable powers of recovery – he had only been down once before in his career and from a less hurtful blow – when the bell signalled the end of the round. Referee Tommy Little's count had reached four. A later rule change, introduced by the medical men, might have caused Ali's downfall. A count must now continue in any round, except the last, even if the bell interrupts the count. To Ali the Wembley bell must have sounded like an orchestra. He slumped back to his corner where he was doused with water and had his face slapped by an angry Angelo Dundee who had repeatedly warned Ali that Cooper's hook deserved his respect. Dundee also played out what has now become the most distorted and exaggerated act of a big-fight. He rightly called the referee's attention to Ali's split right glove – a tear along the seam of the thumb – from which the horse hair stuffing was pro-truding. The impression given by Cooper supporters, and by those who enjoy the fiction that goes with the fight racket, is that Dundee deliberately tore the glove to give his bemused boxer time to recover.

If it were true I would hail Dundee as the mastermind of all time. Dishonest act, yes. But magnificent just the same. But the myth must be exploded before it grows with time. The truth is that Ali's glove split through natural causes in the *third* round and there are photos showing the hair flying from the glove.

I was seated in the front row facing the royal box and in front of the late Andy Cunningham, chief inspector of the Boxing Board of Control, and the then secretary, Teddy Waltham. They had a quick discussion before the finish of the third round and Cunningham, or an aide, rushed to find a replacement glove. It was delivered to Ali's corner before the end of the fourth though there was no instruction for the glove to be changed until the referee ordered it.

Dundee seized the opportunity to hold up the proceedings but the time interval – confirmed by a BBC television recording – between the end of the fourth and start of the fifth round was only 1 min. 35 secs. So Dundee's action had 'stolen' an extra 35 seconds for Ali. It may well not have been possible to cut off the protective tapes and laces of a glove and retie the replacement within the specified sixty seconds, and extra-time is permitted under these exceptional circumstances.

If Cooper had planted his punch earlier in the round he must have had more than an even chance of finishing Ali. Cooper rarely let opponents off the hook. Ali has quietly and convincingly argued with me that he would have 'waltzed Cooper around and hung on until my head cleared. I swear I'd recovered even before I sat on the stool.'

Certainly Ali's recovery was complete in the fifth when he did not fail to miss Cooper with a single punch. The accurate flow of blows and not an accidental headclash reopened the scar tissue over Cooper's eye. When the blood start to cascade down Henry's face the referee acted quickly and with compassion. There was no way Cooper could have continued though he was unruffled. The bloodflow was a ghastly sight.

Ali had lifted an actor's crown prop from the wardrobe of the London Palladium where the weigh-in ceremony took place. He wore the crown on his way into the ring. He was cheered or jeered according to the acceptance of his acting arrogance. But he dismissed the offer of wearing the crown when he left the ring. He would not overplay the part at the expense of a bloodied and popular loser.

Their second meeting happened in May 1966, when Ali came back to Britain as champion, to risk his real crown against Cooper. It was the most spectacular and emotional night in British heavyweight history. They fought on another soccer pitch, Highbury, the London home of Arsenal Football Club.

Jack Solomons had staged the first fight with all his promotional flair. Rival Harry Levene, in conjunction with Viewsport Closed-circuit Ltd, staged the second with bull and blare. The promotion took £212,000 at the gate, this was a higher figure than the Wembley gate money for the World Cup soccer final a few months later.

The fight was not recorded by either BBC or ITV. It was the first big-fight of the era to be banned from the home screens, except for now defunct Pay-TV which operated with a coin in the slot in the Southwark and Westminster areas.

I commentated for the £2 viewers and the string of cinemas that showed the fight throughout Britain. Again the fight was evenly fought for six rounds with Ali backing off, sliding out of corners, and never seeking to clown. He had learned the lesson from the first fight. But again Cooper's eyebrow proved vulnerable. The tissues had not hardened during the intervening three years. His brow ripped open like a zip fastener and he was again prevented from fighting on without having shown the slightest sign of being put down or, indeed, of being beaten.

Ali's seven fights in the two years after becoming champion

29

ranged from brilliant to degrading. He tortured Floyd
Patterson for twelve rounds in Las Vegas, and I do not consider that Ali 'carried' Patterson because the champion threw
his arms in a boxers salute of victory in the sixth round when
he thought Patterson had collapsed. Patterson stayed a further
six rounds because he was stubbornly brave despite being
wracked with pain from a muscular spasm of his back. The
referee, I believed, had allowed Patterson to linger too long.

George Chuvalo, the india-rubber Canadian, slogged 15-
rounds with Ali in Toronto and defied all efforts to floor
him. Chuvalo was impervious to punishment; the bravest
fighter of his era.

Brian London offered token resistance for only three rounds
against Ali at Earls Court in 1966 – Brian's brother, Jack,
did not even bother to climb into the ring to assist his
stricken relation.

German Karl Mildenberger, a dour southpaw, gave Ali a
worthwhile fight in Frankfurt a month later. Ali repeatedly
says Mildenberger, who lasted twelve rounds, gave him the
hardest fight. We suspect Ali is being generous because the
two battles with Frazier were much tougher. But because of
continuous training and a three-fight schedule in four months
he looked weary and was laborious against the German.

Ali's peak fight was probably dismissing Cleveland
Williams, a huge, muscled Texan, in three rounds two months
after meeting Mildenberger. Ali was superb and hitting with
venom at the Houston Astrodome on November 14, 1966.
Big Cat Williams, who carried a bullet in his belly, was put
out in three rounds.

Zora Folley, a gentleman boxer with a sporting print style,
was Ali's final opponent as champion. Folley was k.o.'d in
style in seven rounds.

Ali's taunting of Ernie Terrell in 1967 in 15-rounds of
spite is not my favourite memory of the master at work. It
was sickening to watch Ali goading the gangling Terrell,
one-time WBA champion, and yelling 'What's my name?'

Terrell, like Frazier later, had insisted on calling Ali by his known name of Cay.

Ali, of course, had every right to change his name – like Jersey Joe Walcott or even Joe Louis who dropped the Barrow surname. Even Ali's idol, Sugar Ray Robinson, had a borrowed name.

Ali sent the shock waves through the hard hats of America when he declared his intention of refusing to be drafted for the atrocious Vietnam war. 'I don't have nothing against them Viet Cong. They never called me nigger' he said. 'If I have to die I'll die fighting for freedom here.'

It began Ali's political persecution, although there were thousands hiding in Canada and in college campuses to dodge the draft, and politicians were not being asked to re-sign their seats because of similar opposition to the war. Ali found himself despised because he was a spokesman for peace.

Later on, the opposition to the futile war escalated, as American casualties mounted, and Ali began to be accepted as a symbol of right, youth and blackness winning 'Right On's' from youngsters of all colours.

When the time came for Ali to step forward at the Houston service induction centre he refused and said 'I have searched my conscience and I find I cannot be true to my belief in my religion by accepting such a call.' He claimed his right as a Muslim minister to become a conscientious objector. A pacifist held the post of world champion in the most brutal sport!

In a rush to prove their patriotism the New York Commission and the World Boxing Association stripped Ali of his title within hours of him refusing the call up. Ali was tried in Houston, found guilty, and sentenced to five years in prison and a fine of 10,000 dollars.

Budd Schulberg, author, fight bug and Ali admirer, wrote. 'Unlike businessmen we have known who were convicted of multi-million dollar frauds but were allowed to carry on their business as usual until the final dispensation of their cases, Ali was deprived of his licence and prohibited from practising his trade.'

An attempt to let Ali fight abroad was met by the cancelling of his passport. The WBA organised a hurried elimination tournament to find Ali's successor and Jimmy Ellis, a Kentucky crony and sparring partner of Ali's, came out the winner. Ellis had only been accepted to make up the number with Floyd Patterson, Jerry Quarry, Leotis Martin and Thad Spencer.

Ali spent his time, pending appeal against sentence, lecturing and trying to establish Champburger chain shops. He was steadily going broke. There was a time in Miami when Ellis hired Ali to spar with him. Ali also had a publicity workout against Joe Bugner.

After three wasted years at the physical peak of his life Ali won the legal battle. Seven Supreme Court judges ruled that the boxing commissions were wrong to have deprived Ali of his livelihood. His sentence was quashed.

He came back with a bang in the *Gone With The Wind* country of Atlanta, Georgia. We lined up with Georgians on People's Day at the State Governor's office to ask Lester Maddox, who had been known to clobber trouble shooters with an axe handle, if he approved of Ali's comeback. Maddox was opposed to a draft dodger being permitted to wage ruled ring war in Atlanta. But Maddox was playing politics and needed the growing black vote.

Ali took on Jerry Quarry, a Californian of Irish descent, on October 26, 1970. It was the first time that blacks appeared to outnumber whites at a big fight in the States. The Ali comeback, with a celebration in the air, charged us with excitement that no other heavyweight had been able to generate.

The fight was an anti-climax and inconclusive. Quarry was badly cut on the face and stopped in three rounds. It needed a fight that took Ali into the 15th round, against bold Oscar Bonavena of Argentine, to convince us that Ali was almost as good as his youth. Bonavena had not previously been knocked out. But Ali put him down three times in the final round – the typical grandstand finish. Under New York ruling Bonavena was automatically stopped when going down a third time in the same round.

Ali was then ripe, he thought, to regain the crown from Joe Frazier who had slaughtered Ellis. The showdown fight, the first between unbeaten heavyweight champions, was the costliest sporting event of all time. It was all about big money and ego. Ali and Frazier were paid over one million pounds each. Ali, typically, called it 'the biggest sporting event in the history of the whole planet earth'.

It took place at boxing's shrine, Madison Square Garden, New York, on March 8, 1971. It was exciting and theatrical. I would place it at the top of the heavyweight fights that I have most enjoyed. The atmosphere was overpowering. Reporters were issued with colourful golf caps to be indentified by the battalion of gun-toting security cops to prevent them cracking the wrong heads in case of riot.

Three astronauts were relegated to the sixth row; Frank Sinatra took pictures for a magazine; Burt Lancaster became a commentator; bullfighter El Cordobes was another face in the crowd. Personalities ranged, alphabetically, from Woody Allen to David Frost, Danny Kaye and Andy Williams. There were costumes ranging from brocaded tuxedos, to sequin capes and gaily coloured minks. Salvadore Dali pronounced the occasion as surrealistic.

The wise guys of Broadway circled the arena that spreads from 7th to 8th avenues and had no trouble touting 150 dollar tickets (some 30 rows back) for one thousand dollars. Las Vegas gamblers estimated the fight had generated a billion dollars in bets. Three hundred million TV viewers in 46 countries were looking in. There were 337 closed circuit sites (from cinemas to stadiums and hotel suites) seeing the fight as it happened. Every cinema in Britain was crowded at 3 a.m. With sub-freezing temperatures and a 30 m.p.h.

B

wind, 5,000 people watched an outdoor screen in Pittsburgh.

It was the genuine fight of the century. Ali and Frazier had been kept apart at the weigh in, a move by the Frazier camp to prevent Ali setting up waves of depression by putting the Philadelphia ex-slaughterman, an uncomplicated person, in psychological knots. But Frazier, as it turned out, was totally devoid of fear.

A crowd beseiged the Garden for the mere formality of watching the gladiators going to the scales and Ali, though booked at a hotel only one block away, was unable to get out. Fans flocked to the Garden exits and Ali's handlers feared for his safety. He became a prisoner on a camp bed in a windowless, concrete-walled room for nearly ten hours.

The potentate of his people had fought only 18 serious rounds in the previous four years. During the same period Frazier had fought 73 rounds. They were contrasting characters in their personalities but their character in combat was the strength to trade punches and ignore pain.

From the start graceful Ali moved in, moved out, made an assessment. He could place a punch as delicate as putting a stamp on an envelope. He exposed the clumsiness of thick-thighed Frazier who pummelled his punches in the manner of a dog burrowing for a bone.

Frazier's job was to grind Ali to a standstill. Ali could not resist the show off, the grandstanding, in the desire to both frustrate and belittle Frazier. But Ali's calculated comedy, hoping for Frazier to punch himself out, failed. By the sixth round Ali was ahead as though he was boxing the ears of a disobedient child instead of swopping punches with a 14 st. 9 lb. prize fighter who moved forward like a threshing machine. Ali ignored defence and fed himself to this machine that could pound everything into scrap. He waved his head in placid contempt as if to say 'he's not hurting me'. He absorbed the most fearsome of Frazier's punches. He leaned against the ropes beckoning Frazier to hit him and declared 'It's no contest'.

Yet Frazier, I am convinced, was strong enough to have walked through many of the idolised heavies of yesteryear. His punch-rate was as fast as a lightweight. Frazier countered Ali's fooling by dropping his hands in mimicry and waved Ali on. They looked to be playing patacake, but when the real punches landed they exploded with sickening thuds.

With both foolishly exposing their chins it seemed impossible that they would survive 15-rounds without a count-out. Ali held a glove against Frazier's forehead and eluded punches or frowned over those that landed. But his clowning was staged too early in the fight. Despite the theatricals the pace was too demanding. On my card Ali was ahead after eight rounds but the dramatic change came in the ninth. Frazier's body hitting, it matched any heavyweight in history, forced Ali to box flat-footed.

In the eleventh Frazier's blows had Ali rolling into a corner, a man caught in a violent wave. Frazier had taken the lead. But Ali weathered the storm, with water being tossed at him even before he reached the corner – an act that later brought offender Bundini Brown a suspension in New York – while Angelo Dundee slapped his thighs and issued terse orders.

The fooling was finished. Both fighters' faces began to swell. The punch exchanges became breathtaking. At one stage Frazier complained to his cornermen and looked angrily at the referee. It was yet another dramatic moment. The referee had accidentally poked his finger in Frazier's eye as he prised the fighters out of a clinch.

After the eleventh a doctor checked Ali in his corner, yet he incredibly proved himself, in distress, a greater fighter than in victory. Ali clearly won the fourteenth round with a superb display but his stamina after the lay-off was suspect. His ultimate undoing was trading punches and fighting Frazier's kind of fight.

The points seemed in balance – most British cinema TV viewers reckoned Ali was winning – but after 21 seconds of

35

the final round Frazier fired the last shell of his big left gun. The arcing blow upended Ali, his head ricocheting off the canvas. Few men would have survived such a blow. But Ali is something else and he forced his disobedient legs up at 'three' and was given the mandatory count of eight. The knockdown cemented Frazier's victory yet, incredibly, Ali landed the most punches in the last minute. It was the quality of punch and not the quantity that convinced all three officials that Frazier had won. The club had beaten the spear!

Referee Arthur Mercante had eight rounds Frazier, six Ali, one even – a score matching my own. The judge who voted Frazier eleven rounds to Ali's four was rightly castigated. Ali studied the fight film and argued 'I counted the punches. I landed 688; he landed 388. How could they say I lost?'

Frazier snarled 'I beat him good and he knows it.'

Ali dispensed of his usual post-fight conference and was laid out in the rear seat of a limousine, exhausted and taken to hospital for an X-ray on a feared fractured jaw. His jaw proved sound. But the X-ray plates were stolen as a souvenir.

Frazier, the now undisputed title holder, became a voluntary patient in hospital. He was distressed and demanded a rest. He suffered a kidney ailment.

It took three years to rematch them, and Frazier accepted the return as a non-champion having made the mistake of trying to out-slug George Foreman in Jamaica. Frazier was annihilated in two rounds.

The Ali-Frazier replay, on January 28, 1974, was just as stirring. There were no knockdowns and some may argue that both carried some lead in their legs, but the clash was just as captivating. This time Frazier, who fought like Neanderthal man, was bewildered by Ali's magic. Much of the fight, in the same ring, was fought as though the moves had been choreographed and timing was often slow. But, for three million dollars each, Ali and Frazier showed it was not a veterans night.

It was not all pretty to watch, because there was no pity. 20,748 excited fans dare not take their eyes off the ring or mop their brows. Frazier, 30, was bleeding inside before the first bell and he became careless with his urgency to hook and hack Ali to pieces. Ali looked trim again st 15 st. 2 lb. He toyed with Frazier, punished him. Ali also clung to Frazier to prevent him from sapping Ali's strength by persistently pounding his body.

Ali winked in contempt, did a shuffle, and taunted Frazier with the speed and spite of his blows. Because Ali had never evoked awe in Frazier it became Honest Joe's downfall. Frazier had never taken pride in avoiding punches and by the finish the ex-champion became a beaten, trudging facsimile of himself.

Ali's sense of theatrical and his marvellous grit gave him a finish to remember. He jigged, jabbed, punched, slapped, shoved, and looked positively stimulated by the sight of the swelling on Frazier's face.

Ali later acknowledged his thanks to a predominantly Caucasian audience who had cheered his mastery. The New York Commission refused to allow the decision to be announced until the ring was cleared.

There were still some doubts. Had Frazier's aggression, always eye-catching, overcome Ali's shuffle? My own unsought markings gave Ali the advantage by seven rounds to five, though on British judging, ignoring Frazier's forward march that does not, necessarily, warrant points, I would have scored Ali a slightly larger margin.

The official verdict was unanimous but not a runaway win for Ali. Referee Tony Perez made it 6–5 with one round even. The judges were 7–4 with one even, and 8–4 for Ali.

We await part three of the great serial. It is the fight most likely to bring Ali his biggest reward as the new champion. But there are other easier pickings. World No. 3 Ron Lyle, a Liston-like fighter with a prison record, was ahead of the queue, but lost an obscure fight in Honolulu.

European champion, Joe Bugner, with time on his side, could be Ali's long-range and, maybe, the curtain closing opponent. George Foreman is stuck on the sidelines and waits to be recalled.

Bugner, the white beefcake champion, has qualified for a second chance by giving Ali a full course engagement during his bread-and-butter earning period as non-champion. They fought at Las Vegas in 1973 and, despite being cut over the left eye in the opening round, Bugner finished twelve. The Hungarian-born adonis from Huntingdonshire was a handsome loser on points but visiting fans celebrated that he had at least finished the course and had not been off his feet. It was comparable, it seemed, to celebrating Dunkirk as a victory, but there was merit in Bugner's showing. Bugner's manager, Andy Smith, accepted the fight for his big hope because there was a sign that Ali had found fighting a chore and that he was ready to retire. Smith did not want Bugner to miss a chance of at least being able to say he shared the ring with the Greatest. Some argue that Bugner survived by courtesy of half-hearted Ali, but Ali had whipped himself into respectable shape for the fight and privately admitted that he did not regard Bugner as an easy touch.

Bugner's physique and style are ideally suited to giving Ali concern. Bugner is seven years younger than Ali and he can afford to dwell and hope that Ali is shorn of reflex when, or if, they meet again with the title at stake.

Ali slackened training after defeating Bugner and he was not tuned-up for a fight against an ex-Marine, Ken Norton, five weeks later. It was the Ali shock fight, and took place in Norton's adopted home town of San Diego. The no-hoper was adjudged a twelve-rounds points winner. It was a split vote, but there was no debate about the broken jaw that Ali suffered in the second round.

Fight traders who had been ready to deride Ali admired

him when the chips were down. He fought bravely and without complaining. Norton proved to be under-rated and probably deserved his victory, but even with a pained jaw Ali fought to a photo finish. Some were quick to write Ali off – I was not one of them. Ali loved the challenge to come back again. With his jaw wired he still managed to make it clear that Norton could not get away with catching him unprepared.

Six months later Ali fought Norton in Los Angeles. Again it was a thrilling fight. Ali had disciplined his mind and body at his own camp at Deer Lake, Pennsylvania. Norton had the guts and guile to make it a second close-call. Ali gained his revenge – but only just – with a twelve-rounds points decision. The mouth won by a whisker!

Norton, was later wrecked by Foreman, and turned to film acting but with Ali back at the top he is entitled to call for a third, showdown match. It could happen.

Ali has come a long way since weighing-in at 7 lb. on January 17, 1942. His mother, Odessa, who was there at the time, says Cassius's first words were 'Gee, Gee'. He was obviously warming up to say 'Gee, I'm the Greatest'. He began boxing, at 12, under the tutelage of a black, Fred Stoner, and a white policeman, Joe Martin, because his bicycle was stolen and he wanted to sort out the thieves.

He won every available amateur title. He captured an Olympic Gold in 1960 by eliminating three superb amateurs, Schatkov of Russia, Madigan of Australia, and Pietryzkowski of Poland. This was probably the finest ring achievement of any amateur boxer.

Having avenged the only two, disputed points losses of his pro career, Ali, the foremost debater of our time, is running out of points to prove.

Whether or not he will succeed in his role as a liberator only time will tell.

2

Joe Louis

'The truths of our youths often become falsehoods in our middle years. It is the fee we pay for being alive. We tolerate leniently, the rotting of the flesh and the defeat of beauty, but it is harder to accept the decay of ideals.

'So I am grateful I am still able to admire Joe Louis for what he was. We were young together and he has survived in my estimation. It is because he was a symbol of force for good, and because he is a decent man.'

The description by American Jimmy Cannon, whom I knew well, speaks for us all. Cannon died in 1973, but the friend of his youth lives on – and will probably hate me for saying it : Joe Louis is a living legend.

He was an historic heavyweight champion. He improved the game and/or the business of boxing by his presence. To the thinking professional, Joe Louis had it all. Even the opponents whom Louis slaughtered both respected and liked him – almost without exception. Louis is a simple man with little education, but the truths he uttered during his heyday gave him a kind of radiance. He was never known to seek the sanctuary of a lie.

Louis held the world heavyweight championship from 1937 and made a record 25 successful defences of the title until he was dethroned by a vastly under-rated Ezzard Charles in 1950. Though he did not gain the championship until 1937 Louis was generally considered to be the uncrowned champion from 1935 when he thrashed the giant Italian Primo Carnera in six rounds and knocked out the powerful adonis, Maxie Baer, in four.

He was unquestionably, the most complete heavyweight of them all. Doyen writer, Peter Wilson, who saw many of Louis's fights, rates him the greatest ever. Younger Harry Carpenter, BBC commentator, describes Louis as *the* master of boxing in his lifetime.

Though six men managed to put Louis down – maybe the slightest flaw in his greatness – he was beaten only three times. And two of those losses came when Louis was too old for fighting. Louis's boxing, in one sense, was unspectacular. He was not the flashy footwork type. They tagged him 'The Brown Bomber' and 'Shufflin' Joe'. Fleet-footed opponents however, found that Joe's cagey shuffling cut down the area of the ring available for them to manoeuvre. The power he packed looked capable of lopping a man's head from his shoulders. He was the most correct hitter I have seen and he turned the destruction of his opponents into an art form.

Louis's left-jab was a shortened version of the much-vaunted English-style straight left and it proved more punishing. Using his left jab he could set up his victim for either a lethal left-hook, delivered with unerring accuracy, or for the text book right cross.

Louis did his job with a cold detachment, fighting with a deadpan expression that never changed in victory or defeat. Yet Joe swears that he never hated anybody. He could get angry, yes, but angry to the point of hate, never. He was so superbly equipped for his craft that he never needed glib phrases planted in his mouth by publicity-seeking promoters. Everything Louis did – in and out of the ring – had dignity.

It is generally accepted that Joe Louis created more goodwill for the negro race than any other athlete, and I think the claim is true that he was hero worshipped by almost as many white people as black. Yet Louis had a liberal sprinkling of white and a larger splash of Indian blood. His background is fascinating.

He was born Joseph Louis Barrow in the Buckalew mountain country of Alabama, near Lafayette, on May 13, 1914. The name Barrow traces back to a rich pre-civil war landowner, James Barrow, who was reputed to be the owner of hundreds of slaves. He was Joe's great-great-grandfather. Hence the white strain. The Indian blood is Cherokee because Joe's grandmother was Victoria Harp Barrow, granddaughter of Charles Hunkerfoot, a full-blooded Indian chief. The Bomber has first cousins in the Southern cotton fields today who could pass easily for Indian braves or Indian princesses with their lithe, erect bodies, high cheekbones and straight black hair.

Joe was born on the farm of Peter Sheley, an uncle on his mother's side, who had rented the farm to Monroe 'Mun' Barrow to raise crops. Only the chimney stack of the squalid cabin where Joe was born, the seventh of a family, now remains.

'Mun' Barrow, Joe's father, was the son of Lon and Victoria Harp Barrow. Lon's wife and sister, Susan, belonged to a prominent half breed, James Harp, a wealthy planter and slave owner. Susan was the daughter of Chief Hunkerfoot who, like most chieftains, had inter-married with slave women whom white planters had previously selected as prize specimens.

So the mass of Barrows living on farms where 'the stars fell thickest in Alabama' are a distinctly mixed race with little African blood remaining.

'Us is a proud family of folks' one of the eldest Barrows has said, 'Our forebears were born in slavery and you know how it was then with the good looking mulatto women. We got the best white blood of the State in our veins and the best Indian blood, too.'

Joe was only two when his father, who stood 6 ft. 3 in. and weighed 190 lb., broke under the strain of the grinding toil and ceaseless worry of trying to support a growing family on meagre earnings. He was sent to the State hospital for the insane and never came out.

For several years, Lillie, Joe's mother, fought a discouraging battle to keep her brood alive. Then she married Patrick Brooks, a widower, who had a large flock of his own bringing the family to thirteen. It was Brooks who persuaded the family to leave the dirt farms and go to Detroit where jobs were available at the Ford plant. On borrowed money the Barrows set out for their new Utopia. Joe was only twelve and the rough Michigan city was the most complete contrast imaginable to the cottonfields. It induced a shyness in young Joe which affected his speech, but this didn't matter for a manual job at the famous car factory. To this day, if things become gloomy, Joe will quip that, anyway they still keep his job open at Fords. Mrs Barrow wanted her proud son to become a violinist, but it was not with a bow but boxing blows that his hands were to win him fame.

At 16, Joe Louis laced on his first boxing glove merely as a favour to a friend, Thurston McKinney, who was winning contests as an amateur, and wanted somebody to act as a sparmate.

He proved to have a natural aptitude and Joe was encouraged to enter amateur competitions. But Joe was not an instant success. Johnny Miller, Joe's first opponent, knocked him down seven times but Joe lasted the three rounds distance. He learned the hard way.

He then made a strange discovery. Boxing was the easiest way to overcome shyness! The successful use of his fists enabled him to walk as tall as the other youths.

In 54 bouts, including Golden Gloves and AAU tournaments, Louis lost only four decisions. He scored 41 knockouts or stoppages. All this time Joe had managed to keep his boxing prowess a secret from his mother, but when it came to championship time she had to know. Mrs Barrow could not stop her boy from seeking glory and battling his way out of Detroit's ghetto. The heavyweight title is still the shortest distance between poverty and plenty.

It was in 1934, when he was 20, that Joe decided it was time to get paid for his pains. He approached a local drug store owner, John Roxborough, and asked him to become his manager. Later Roxborough took Julian Black as a partner and jointly they handled Louis for 16 years, though it was New York promoter, Mike Jacobs, once a 'ticket scalper', who had the biggest influence on Louis's career. Roxborough and Black, both negroes, were new in the fight business but they were astute enough to hire Jack (Chappie) Blackburn, an ex-fighter, to become Louis's trainer. Blackburn was a hard, fight-wise man who had run into trouble with the law, but he coached Louis brilliantly to become, in the opinion of many shrewd judges, the greatest of them all.

Louis won the world championship at 23 (then the youngest-ever) and his 25 defences doubled those of all previous holders of the heavyweight title. He made seven defences within a single year and had seven defences attracting crowds among the top 32 in boxing history at all weights. By knocking out 22 of 25 challengers his average 'kill' was six and a half rounds.

Only one opponent out of 71, Max Schmeling, a German of considerable boxing ability, punch power and undoubted bravery, was able to humble Louis in the prime of his youth. It was not until Louis had become an ageing lion, at 37, that he was knocked out by Rocky Marciano. That was Louis's last fight.

I have a film of Louis's two most painful defeats. The stripling Louis, a month past his 22nd birthday, was caught in round twelve by a long, fierce and accurate right hander from Schmeling. Then nine years Louis's senior, Schmeling had won the world heavyweight championship in 1930 – the only time the big title was taken with a foul blow.

Louis rushed into a match beyond his capacity. With the advantage of hindsight it is clear that many of the shrewdest judges of the game have been justified in rating Schmeling as one of the top ten heavies of all time.

'I made the fight tough for myself' Louis has said. 'He didn't really make it tough for me. He did so many wrong things, but I couldn't go get him. It was a lousy fight. I saw him making mistakes but I stood and watched. I dried out and dieted too much and took four pounds off the day before the fight. Its a lousy excuse, it was just a lousy fight. But my machine wasn't running that night. I weighed 211 lb. and should have been 5 lb. heavier. But don't make no mistakes, Schmeling was a hell of a fighter.'

The match with Schmeling was premature but it had some justification. Nobody thought that a Louis who had half murdered the awesome Primo Carnera could possibly be caught by the lighter German. Certainly I couldn't imagine it. I used to unpack Carnera's training kit every day when it was brought home by my father, Dick, who, with his twin brother, Jack, was teaching the Italian giant in 1933 at London's St Bride's Institute. Carnera was truly enormous, his ring boots were size 16!

The Italian later held the world heavyweight championship and, when dethroned, was pitted against Louis to measure the Bomber's progress. Carnera stood 6 ft. 5¾ in. and weighed 18 st. 2 lb. The fight took place at Louis's first appearance at the Big Apple – slick, cynical New York – where 62,000 crammed into the Yankee Stadium on a humid June 25, 1935 – the year in which Louis had flattened eight of ten opponents.

Louis massacred Carnera in six rounds. A distinguished sportswriter, Paul Gallico, later to become a boxing abolitionist, reported, 'It was the most technically brilliant piece of planned destruction I have ever witnessed.'

Louis had listened to orders and was content to bide his time, circling the Ambling Alp and pecking him bloody with his left hand. The crowd began to yawn. The killer from Detroit they thought, was a flash in the pan. The softening up process worked, Louis watched his prey, wary but confident, much as the game warden waits for the elephant he has drugged, to topple. Then, in a few awesome moments, the seeming indolent Louis sprang into action and, in the words of Gallico 'transformed a brawny, courageous man into a babbling goggle-eyed jelly'.

Louis's blows were the hardest that one man can conceivably deliver to another. The giant's body, incredulous that such force could be mustered against it, began to quiver.

It was as though Louis had undertaken to poleaxe a bull with his fists. Carnera was a brave man, but the combination of Louis's blows, delivered with such speed and with near perfect accuracy, brought Carnera to his knees in round six. He was bravely trying to clamber up when referee Arthur Donovan threw himself mercifully in front of Louis and signalled that the fight was over. From that moment, New York, capital of America's pugilism, took the super Joe Louis to its hustling heart.

The shock defeat by Schmeling had not only hurt young Joe's pride but threatened to hinder his earnings. 'A guy fights for dough, except maybe once,' Louis said, 'Get me Schmeling at any price.'

But while the wheeling and dealing went on and Schmeling's advisers, said to include a certain Herr. A. Hitler, were playing the waiting game, Louis's counsellors came up with a better idea. Joe could win the world championship and *then* fight Schmeling. The title holder, at the time, was the much loved James J. Braddock and since a negro had not been permitted a crack at the world's supreme prize in twenty-years, it was not easy to arrange such a match.

Braddock was the Cinderella Man who came off the breadline to be fed – as a pushover – against the powerful Maxie Baer. He ended up clobbering Baer to become the heaviest underdog title winner of all time. Braddock revealed to me recently that he was born in Manchester, England, where his father was a policeman, and not along the Hudson River, USA. (James J. passed away in 1974.)

Braddock's manager, Joe Gould, knew that Louis would hammer Braddock and while he held the title reins, Gould drove a hard bargain. Braddock and the manager were to receive a percentage of all Louis's title defences in the event of him defeating Braddock. Otherwise they would find other challengers for Braddock and give Louis the runaround. The fight was eventually signed to take place at Comiskey Park, Chicago, on June 22, 1937.

Braddock, though knowing he would be compensated by Louis in defeat, did not seek quittance or a runaway. His was a magnificent losing stand. Braddock had only one more fight after Louis, his 85th, outpointing Tommy Farr in New York in 1938.

Louis had lived down the prejudice which a great mass of Americans had retained since Jack Johnson had beaten the 'unbeatable' white man, Jim Jeffries, in 1910. Liberal minded Americans did not like to be reminded of the tawdry farce of a search for a 'White Hope' and they remembered the 19 deaths, including lynchings, that had followed the triumphs of the first black champion. The easiest solution was unofficially to ban 'mixed' fights for the world heavyweight title. But the people yearned for Louis, graceful, crushing, Louis, to gain revenge over the Black Uhlan Schmeling.

Louis had been fed seven opponents of varying shapes and sizes to knock over and so regain the kind of confidence he needed to thrash the needling German who was reported to have been making racial slurs. It has been established that Schmeling was not responsible for those jibes. The words were attributed to him by Nazi propagandists. Schmeling was undoubtedly used by the Hitler regime as an exemplar of Aryan prowess. He hotly denies that he was a registered member of the Nazi Party, though he served with the crack Nazi paratroopers.

Louis has considered that the night he put his punches together in a totally satisfactory way was against Al Ettore in Philadelphia. Ettore is rarely mentioned in the Louis saga. Jack Sharkey, a previous holder of the world title, was k.o.'d in three rounds. Jorge Brescia, Eddie Simms, Stan Ketchel, Bob Pastor and Nate Brown, were the other members of the not so magnificent seven. Pastor managed to stay the full ten rounds.

The night Louis met Braddock he was, conceivably, the best heavyweight of all time. There were, however, some whoops of delight in the first round when Braddock used the ropes in a catapult movement to land a twisting upper-cut, part hook, which dropped Louis. The Bomber's legs sagged and he required a rest of a 'two' count. Louis, it was clear, would have to respect the 'old champion' – though at 32, Braddock was not exactly senile.

Braddock considers he fought his best against Louis, (including the win over Baer), but nothing he could do would stop the Bomber in full flight. With 14 st. 1 lb. behind them Braddock's punches did not lack power and often his jab would jolt Louis. But Joe was ruthlessly softening up Braddock for the classic kill. It came in the eighth round. A left to the body brought Braddock's head forward and with a right-hander, still remembered for its velocity, Louis knocked Braddock down. He crumbled slowly as though he were being dismantled piece by piece. 'I couldn't have got up if they had offered me a million dollars,' Braddock has said.

Braddock was stuck with the scars of that fight – one of them a matchstick-thin slit through his top lip. So the world got a black champion and in the thirty-seven years that have followed there have been only two white ones – Marciano and Ingemar Johansson.

While Schmeling was being baited for a return fight, Britain's Tommy Farr was given a crack at Louis. Those of us who listened to the crackly radio account of that fight from New York in August 1937, well remember the drama.

Many of us knew that Farr, from Tonypandy, was rock hard and wily as well – information which was stupidly disregarded by critics in America. They believed that Farr was a mere pushover. How they ate their words!

In the history of British boxers going West to seek fame and fortune, none deserved the fame more than Farr. He matched Louis for wits, absorbed the champion's best punches and valiantly pegged away. Louis could not halt Farr – and he knew it. The face-saving suggestion was made by some Americans that Louis was fighting at half-throttle. Nothing is farther from the truth. Farr *worried* Louis. Years of experience, plus fighting up from the middleweights in the Welsh boxing booths, had made Farr a ring craftsman. All he lacked was the only thing that mattered – a finishing dig.

After 15-rounds of brain to match the brawn, Louis was declared the points winner – a decision that Farr, to his credit, has never doubted. But as the years roll on, the story tellers of that memorable fight tend to make the points margin shorter than it actually was and even suggest that Farr may have been robbed.

It was good enough that Farr had performed so creditably without depriving Louis of his glory. It was probably Farr's best fight. Louis had better fights, but he could only perform as well as the opposition allowed. Louis and Farr, and their wives, have met in recent years and dined while they recalled the battle of '37. 'Just talking about that fight still makes my nose bleed,' laughs Farr. 'Tahmmy,' says Joe, 'Was a real smart guy. Nobody's fool. I didn't carry nobody. I just couldn't catch up with Farr.'

That fight, more than any other, convinced Louis that racial prejudice had ended. His advisers had feared that if Louis failed to knock out a white man he could not expect to get the points decision. They were wrong.

In Louis's 34 wins before he gained the title, only five

opponents were there to hear the final bell. But there was still one old score to settle – one that really mattered. It was the chance to fight Schmeling again.

Schmeling was tempted into action – exactly one year after Louis had won the title on June 22, 1938. The fight was at the Yankee Stadium, New York, and the weather was sultry as befitted the occasion. It was perhaps, the most dramatic championship fight of all time. Hitler had sent a cable to Schmeling addressed 'to the next heavyweight champion of the world'. Schmeling lost his crown to Jack Sharkey – subsequently annihilated by Louis in 1932 – and it was a Schmeling turned 33 who faced Louis for the second time.

To have licked Louis was one thing, but to have gloated over the achievement was something else. For the first and only time in training Louis uttered a threat, 'I'm fighting Hitler's man,' he told reporters at Pompton Lakes training camp, 'In Germany they have ridiculed me and my race. You wanna make a little money? Go bet I'll tear his head off in one round. Yep, one round.'

That was quite a speech from the least loquacious champion in history.

Louis, the placid professional, had declared his antagonism in burning personal terms. It seemed that he could barely wait to unload his carefully nurtured hate upon the bristled chin of Schmeling – the man Hitler had declared to be the symbol of Aryan supremacy over all other kinds of men.

Louis was in the full flush of his powers and was itching for both personal and racial revenge.

The atmosphere was electric around the floodlit ring as the opening bell sounded. At once Schmeling sought to reproduce the punch that had undone Louis two years before. Fractionally, however, he misjudged his distance and the mistake was incorrectable. Louis denied him even a fraction of a second in which recovery might have been possible.

Louis punched the German with a controlled, but overwhelming salvo to the head. Pinned to the ropes, Schmeling's only effective resistance was to stoop and seek the shelter of the ropes. But Louis put every ounce of 200 lbs. behind his right and drove it to Schmeling's jaw.

Schmeling was a brave man but courage is irrelevant when assault surpasses the tensile strength of flesh, bone and nerve. He half-turned into the ropes, trying to regain control of his legs, and in doing so, his left side was wide open. Louis was right on top of him and picked his spot for the next blow – a right to the body. The impact made Schmeling cry out involuntarily. Hard bitten fight followers call it a squeal. When I watch that punch on film I still quiver as though Louis had hit me. Not one of that 70,000 crowd – a million dollar attendance – will ever forget it.

Instinctively, yet pathetically, Schmeling aimed a retaliatory right, but again the German was hit by body blows that threatened to collapse his rib cage. Then a shorter blow to the jaw dropped him for a count of 'three'. A pulverising left hook, a Louis special, followed, and sent him on his back for 'two'. It seemed incredible that Schmeling could climb off the canvas again – but he did. Then a crushing right to the point of the jaw sent him toppling again. The towel of surrender fluttered into the ring. Referee Arthur Donovan abandoned his count at eight, having ignored the towel, and flung his arms wide to signify that the massacre was over and that Louis stood avenged.

'I stopped it to prevent Schmeling being killed,' said Donovan. The time : 2 min. 4 secs.

Of course, there was the usual inquests, and post-mortems. Schmeling was bundled off to the Polyclinic Hospital to nurse his hurts and to complain that he had been fouled when Louis's right crashed into his kidneys.

The German Ambassador lodged a formal protest with the U.S. State Department and Schmeling sailed home to Europe on a stretcher. Herr Hitler was not amused.

The personal spite has long since died between Louis and

Schmeling. They have met on numerous occasions since that unforgettable clash.

In 1972, when Louis was hospitalised in Denver, his old rival, now a prosperous mink farmer and chief sales representative of Pepsi-Cola in Germany, visited him and left quietly after paying the bulk of Louis's hospital bills. So much for the hate campaign of the thirties.

Louis's career went on for 31 fights after his victory over Schmeling. But the war years, with Joe a serving soldier, took its toll. He never fully recovered the glory of the thirties. Even so, there were great opponents among Louis's so called 'Bum of the Month' campaigns.

Tony ('I'll moider da bum') Galento, only 5 ft. 9 in., but weighing almost 17 st., (and allegedly training on beer and hamburgers), came along to swipe Louis off his feet with a left hook. He paid the price for taking a liberty with Joe. Louis cut him into ribbons in four rounds.

John Henry Lewis, a light-heavyweight champion who had beaten Len Harvey in London, was reckoned good enough to challenge Louis – but he went out in one round. 'I made it quick 'cos he was my friend,' said Louis.

Buddy Baer, big edition of brother Maxie, was bowled over in the first round, while smart moving Billy Conn played artful dodger until Louis caught up with him in the thirteenth – a fight that brought the famous wry remark from Louis, 'he can run, but he can't hide'. Six years later, when both men were ring-rusty due to their spell in the services, Conn tried his luck again. He lasted only eight rounds.

The smartest boxer Louis ever faced was Jersey Joe Walcott. A shifty boxer and punch feinter. In 1947 he bamboozled a slowing Louis. For the first time in his life, Louis ducked out of a ring to the sound of boos when he was adjudged a 15-rounds points winner. A rematch was inevitable and this time Louis made no mistake. Walcott went out in the eleventh.

It was Ezzard Charles in New York who finally caught a fading Louis at a time when his reflexes were slowing and his paunch was beginning to show. And how they hated poor Charles for capturing the championship. The most under-valued heavyweight of them all, Ezzard could not be forgiven for dethroning the great 'bomber'.

After eight wins, including stopping Lee Savold (who cut up Bruce Woodcock in London), Louis, badly in need of cash, was pitted against an up-and-comer called Rocky Marciano at New York's Madison Square Garden. At 37, Louis was no long the great man of the ring, the champion with the big heart and the matchless artistry.

It was sixteen years since Louis had first come to New York to show his skills. A war had come and gone. He had conquered every good heavyweight in sight, made millions, lost millions – and stayed a hero. His title had gone and his weight was up to 15 st. 2¾ lb. (a stone more than his stripling championship days) but he was still idolised and acclaimed. He made a friendly salute to the 17,241 New York idolators who had fought to buy tickets at the arena between 49th and 50th Streets. It was later torn down for a parking site and 'The Garden' was moved lower downtown to Penn Station.

Marciano was three-inches shorter, had nine-inches less reach and conceded nearly two-stone. Joe had a ridge of fat appearing over the top of his trunks, but the fans still believed he could show 'em. Marciano, after all, was just a swinger though it was conceded that when he brought out the bludgeon, things had a habit of happening.

Louis jockeyed his way safely through seven rounds, his pride forcing him to check Marciano in his tracks. But his punches could not stop the Rock.

In round eight it was Marciano's turn to start landing blows and when Louis failed to duck a left hook which, in his prime he would have countered even before it had finished its course, he was reduced to the indignity of listening to a count of eight as he sat on the seat of his trunks. At Joe's age a blow of that sort doesn't encourage you to jump up for more.

The end of Joe Louis and the end of an era was only one punch away. Marciano unleashed a right hander and Louis took it full force on the head. He reeled backwards, insensible, his once lithe body battered and bowed over the lower strand of rope. His head cracked on the ring apron as startled photographers snatched away their old fashioned plate cameras.

There was a silence impregnated with history. Nobody could really believe that Joe Louis, the one and only, the inimitable Joe Louis, had been knocked out. Marciano recalled that an elderly woman at the ringside yelled, 'You brute!' Fight hardened fans wiped tears from their eyes.

Louis, of course, provided his own superb punch line when a reporter said it was sad to see him knocked out of boxing. 'I've knocked out lots of guys,' he said.

It was to pay a huge bill for income tax that Louis fought Marciano when he knew his best fighting days were over. The tax man had always haunted Louis, even when he had fought Buddy Baer and Abe Simon and donated his purses to Army and Navy relief funds. He made almost five million dollars in seventeen years, splitting 50–50 with his management who paid all expenses.

He was well managed, but ill advised. He lost on investments, gambled heavily on his golf games, and spent money as though it were going out of style.

In 1957 Louis was so heavily in debt to the tax authorities that the compound interest on what he owed would have required him to earn a million dollars a year – just to keep the bill from rising further. Two trust funds, started for his children, were turned over to the internal revenue department of Uncle Sam. Well wishers sent him cheques, but all were returned.

Louis briefly turned to wrestling ('It's better than stealing') but a heart murmur forced him to abandon to a career that many felt was demeaning to a great man.

When Louis collapsed with heart strain in 1960, the U.S. Government relented and dropped their claim. 'We have gotten all we can get from Mr Louis,' they announced, 'His earning days are over.'

Louis remained candidly humorous about his lost fortune and in a strange way he has never been broke. They call Joe 'America's Guest'. Wherever he goes, there is always somebody he wants to pick up the bill.

New York writer, Barney Nagler, staggered us all in 1972 by reporting that Louis had been hospitalised because he had turned to drugs and was suffering from hallucinations. Joe did not bother to fight back. He came out of hospital, at 58, looking sharper than ever – and laughed about the stories. 'Just a little frustration and depression,' he said.

When Louis entered Madison Square Garden to watch the first Ali v. Frazier battle in 1971, cheers for him drowned those given for two Astronauts, Mayor Lindsay, or for Frank Sinatra. The paint chipped on the Garden roof.

Joe took a handkerchief out of his pocket and dabbed his nose. 'It's nice of them to remember me,' he said to his wife. 'They've never forgotten you, Joe,' she said.

In 1974 they invited the old Bomber back to the Garden and gave him 10,000 dollars to referee Joe Frazier v. Jerry Quarry. Again his reception was tumultuous, though he left the ring to an embarrassed silence. He was criticised for not stopping the fight quickly enough. 'Joe was lost in the mist of Max Schmeling,' they said. It was the last time Joe Louis was expected to be seen in the ring.

He is to be seen sporting a red jacket and golf cap acting as host – they call it a greeter – at Caesars Palace, Las Vegas. I confess I always shake his hand in awe.

3

Sugar Ray Robinson

At his trade Sugar Ray Robinson was a proud, arrogant artist, as close to perfection as any boxer I have seen. Possessed of grace, style, rhythm and good looks, he was able to execute every punch in the book – and, when provoked, a few not in any book. Sugar's pride and vanity were his biggest commercial asset but his greatness lay in the gameness that backed his superb skill. He was never knocked out in twenty years – twenty years that included unlisted bootleg battles, and *nineteen* world championship fights. The man was a marvel. He was a gritty competitor often acclaimed and despised simultaneously by his opponents. They all acknowledged his craft but they also resented being forced to take the cheap end of the prize money for the privilege of sharing a ring with Sugar Ray. He was a star with the trick of relegating his opponents to the role of bit players.

He won the world welterweight 10 st. 7 lb. (147 lb.) championship in 1946, defended it five times, including beating the flashy, classy Cuban Kid Gavilan out of sight, and then vacated the throne. It had taken Robinson six years of campaigning to get his first crack at a world title, during which time he defeated the formidable Fritzie Zivic (twice); fought a brutal five fight series (winning 4–1) against ferocious Jake La Motta; and outpointing three-time world champion, Henry Armstrong.

Robinson, as it turned out, also made the mistake of twice boxing rings around the capable Marty Servo who held the

10 st. 7 lb. title during the forties. Servo was managed by Al Weill (later to launch the unbeaten career of Rocky Marciano). Servo, who died tragically in 1969, proved an honest champion. He retired rather than face Sugar Ray Robinson after holding the welter title for nine months. Tommy Bell, a New Yorker who contested the claim to the vacated crown fought and lost to Robinson during Xmas week, in New York.

The trade had known for years that snake-hipped Sugar, of Harlem, was the best boxer, *and* the best fighter in the division. Sugar was sidestepped, thrown in with the ring brawlers, given the cheap end of the deals. But he survived because he possessed that intangible quality of 'class'. But for an unlucky circumstance he would surely have equalled the feat of Bob Fitzsimmons, (whom I think Robinson could have whipped with one hand), or that of the incredible all-action Henry Armstrong – the feat of winning a world championship at three weights. His ill luck was to be competing against an opponent $15\frac{1}{2}$ lb. heavier on the hottest night in New York history. Sugar melted with heat exhaustion on his corner stool at the close of the thirteenth round. Robinson's record shows that he was beaten inside the distance for the only time in 202 fights by Joey Maxim but it was not regarded as a technical k.o. in boxing's accepted sense. Robinson could 'make' 157 lb. but challenged on June 25, 1942, for the light-heavyweight (174 lb.) championship held by Maxim – a smart, durable boxer who had dethroned Britain's Freddie Mills and was the first to defeat heavyweight Floyd Patterson. The open air battle was postponed for twenty-four hours because of storms that made the humidity of Manhattan insufferable. At such times it is exhausting enough to amble along a sidewalk, taking breathers from one air-conditioned shop entrance to another without having to climb into a fiercely arc-lit twenty-foot square ring. The weigh-in, on the scheduled date, made Robinson 160 lb. to Maxim's $174\frac{1}{2}$ lb. The boxers did not re-weigh on the second day. It meant by fight-time that Maxim must have outweighed Robinson by 20 lb. or more. It was a physical endurance ordeal beyond anything Robinson could have imagined. Maxim was no mug. He could box, he was brave, and he was big and, if it helped, he had the counselling of Jack 'Doc' Kearns behind him.

The Yankee Stadium gate, as you would expect for a Sugar Ray appearance, was 421,615 dollars – a record for a light-heavyweight championship. 47,983 fans soaked as though in a communal sauna bath.

Maxim managed to survive the blistering heat of the arclights which gave off 38,500 watts and raised the ring temperature to an unendurable 104 degrees. For the first time during a championship fight a referee (Ruby Goldstein) collapsed and had to be replaced (by Ray Miller) in the eleventh round. Robinson's sharper hitting and mobility had given him what appeared an unassailable lead. Then on the last stretch, sensation and disaster and Sugar's collapse might perhaps be best compared to that of the Queen's classic horse, Devon Loch, which faltered close to the winning line when hats were off for a Royal victory. There was no warning during the thirteenth round that Robinson would be unable to answer the bell for the fourteenth. Inevitably, he was slowing and blowing – but so was champion Maxim. It was Robinson's 137th fight and he was within sight of making post-war Ring history. He could afford to hit and run, or hold. The fight was virtually won. Judge Artie Aidala had Robinson ahead with nine rounds, three for Maxim, and one even. But Sugar simply dissolved in the heat as he was about to see his name go into the ring's roll of honour. His cornermen, Harry Wiley and Peewee Beal doused Sugar with water, rubbed his ears, planted ice packs on his neck. Dr Alex Schiff was also in attendance but collectively and individually they were helpless – the Great One had been beaten by the elements.

Being unable to concede weight *and* win was, perhaps, the

only chink in Sugar Ray's otherwise superb record of 69 amateur wins (40 in the first round!) when he also defeated the magical champion-to-be Willie Pep. His pro total reached 175 victories (109 k.o.'d or halted) and six drawn in a twenty-five year span. He never won or lost by a foul, although he was once ordered out of a Berlin ring for allegedly landing kidney blows. A few hours later, the disqualification decision against Gerhard Hecht – Sugar had to take cover under the ring from missiles thrown by an irate crowd – was changed by the German Boxing Federation to a no contest.

He never remonstrated with a referee or dredged up an alibi.

I have always unhesitatingly named Robinson as the finest pound for pound boxer of all time. Yet poor Sugar could win only one of four fights in Britain! That was one blot on his record that really irked him. Terry Downes, the colourful world middleweight champion who defeated Robinson in London in 1962, has never claimed mastery, even though Downes justly deserved the decision. 'I only beat a man who called himself Sugar Ray Robinson. The real Sugar was finished. But he gave me such a great fight that I can't imagine what it would have been like fighting him at his peak.' Robinson was 42 when he lost to Downes at Wembley and was given an oxygen inhaler during the closing stages of the fight. Coventry-Irishman, Mick Leahy, stole a photofinish points verdict over Robinson in Scotland two years after Sugar's Wembley downfall. It was not a particularly exciting contest, but I considered Robinson had boxed well enough to win. Referee Ike Powell, of Wales, had, however, a habit of giving decisions that made headlines.

But about one fight there was no dispute at all – despite a misleading radio commentary. It was that fight to remember at Earls Court, London, in 1952 when the king of the ring was tamed by Randolph Turpin then officially advertised as 33–1 against outpointing the middleweight champion.

Turpin captured the heart of the nation by conjuring up the strength, stance and punch power to confuse the mighty Robinson who had been barnstorming round the world with eight fights in three months : Miami; Oklahoma City, Paris; Zurich; Antwerp; Berlin; and Liége. It was Robinson's peak period at the weight, though those close to the champion reckon he was travel and party weary. He had certainly lived it up in Europe.

The fight, in a technical sense, was not as great in retrospect as it seemed on the night. There was too much holding, repetition rounds and an absence of knockdowns for the fight to register as a championship classic. As an occasion it was something else. The tension was unbelievable and a spectator, a relation of the promoter, Jack Solomons, collapsed and died of a heart attack. At the close of each early round there was a sigh of relief that Robinson had failed to catch up with the coffee-coloured Turpin. Then as the fight went on it became obvious that Turpin was set to win. By the end of the thirteenth round the packed crowd began singing 'For he's a Jolly Good Fellow' even though the radio listeners were under the impression that the decision was still in doubt. My old friend, W. Barrington Dalby ('Come in Barry') the inter-rounds summariser, accepted the blame for the impression given to listeners by the use of one wrongly chosen word in the heat and excitement of the commentary. Turpin won on points, without any doubt, and had referee Eugene Henderson's 15-rounds scorecard been declared, (making public the official pointing is comparatively new), I am sure his marking in Turpin's favour would have been considerable.

The story goes that on the night of the big fight King George VI was holding a private function at Buckingham Palace. His Majesty was apparently interested in the plight of the British challenger, generally thought to have little hope of waging a successful world title war. The gathering fell silent while the King listened to the round-by-round radio report – until the King in great excitement threw his arms into the air and announced to his guests, 'He's won it, he's won it.' Such was the fervour at all levels of the nation for the humble lad who had been tagged the Leamington Licker – the lad who fourteen years later was to take his own life at the age of 36.

Robinson had trained at Windsor (at the 'Star and Garter' public house – not the Castle!) surrounded by an entourage (a word he preferred to camp) which included 53 suitcases, a valet, a barber and a golf pro. The manager and the trainers did their work, but the only man Robinson needed after the fight was Dr Vincent Niardello who had flown in from New York a few hours before the fight. Niardello inserted eight stitches into Robinson's gashed eyebrow, lectured him about more disciplined conditioning, and sent him to rest in the sun at Cannes. Later he moved to a more Spartan training camp in America. Robinson's ego as well as his eyebrow had been cut but not for long.

Sixty-four days later Randolph Turpin had the doubtful honour of becoming the shortest reigning world middleweight champion. Sugar Ray, although he suffered another brutal eye injury, was champ again.

It happened at the Polo Grounds, New York, when Turpin was halted in a defenceless state only seconds from the finish of the tenth round. But it was Robinson who was really in worse shape. If Turpin could have clutched, taken a mandatory count, or backed away for those vital seconds, the fight could have been over. Robinson was badly cut. It is however the hallmark of a great boxer to be able to end the fight at the right time. A clash of heads at the start of the tenth, opened Robinson's left eyebrow like a zip fastener. Until then, Robinson had treated Turpin respectfully, even cautiously; the action had been interesting rather than exciting. Turpin had been stunned in the second round but had fully recovered and his awkward effective style continued to trouble the challenger.

As they came out for the tenth, referee Goldstein had the fight scored level. The judges had Robinson ahead by one and two rounds respectively. But 23-year-old Turpin looked decidedly the stronger. Now, however, the bloodflow forced Sugar Ray to fight like an enraged octopus. Sensing that his injury was serious enough to prevent him continuing beyond the tenth, he flailed punches, ripping, effective, cutting blows that were rifle-accurate. Turpin was hooked down for a nine count and then lolled drunkenly against the ropes, his arms dangling (an unfortunate mannerism he had shown in previous fights), his chin exposed and reduced to trying merely to roll his head away from the barrage of blows that came his way. Turpin just failed to take advantage of the time that was running out for Robinson. Bravely he tried to stand up, while Robinson used him as a punchbag. Judging from the slow-motion film of the fight, the referee was right. He could not permit Turpin to take another blow. His job was to prevent undue punishment, not to act as timekeeper. Goldstein hauled Robinson off, with Turpin, doubled-up, his hands lowered, the seat of his black satin trunks touching the middle rope, *yet still on his feet*. It was all over.

Camera bulbs flashed and the ring was invaded like some carnival suddenly out of control. The New York cops climbed upon the ring apron to act as sentinels. The British camp hollered injustice and London promoter, Jack Solomons, the man who had built Turpin from a humble Navy cook to box office hero, was enraged. He accused the Americans of 'jobbing' the champion. Certainly a peak-trained Robinson had, for the second time, found Turpin's unorthodox style – the spread stance, clubbing blows and enormous strength at close quarters – more difficult than that of any other rival. There was no hope of a third showdown fight.

The gate receipts at the Polo Grounds, September 12, 1951, were 767,626 dollars (£274,152), a record for a non-heavyweight fight. The attendance was 61,370. Another £35,285 came from the closed-circuit TV and film rights. Robinson, the 11–5 favourite was paid £81,773 (a financial winner as always) with Turpin's share given as £68,145.

Fifteen years later the memorable Cassius Clay/Henry Cooper world heavyweight title fight at Highbury Stadium drew £62,000 less, though this was still a higher take than for the World Cup soccer final, (England *v.* West Germany), at Wembley the same year.

I had seen Robinson toy with a better-than-average Belgian, Jan de Bruin, in Antwerp, and seven years later I went to America expecting the end of a fighter who had become a legend. Robinson had lost his crown, a year earlier, to Carmen Basilio, a Syracuse onion farmer, a steel built man with a jaw to match, brave and very popular. Robinson and Basilio had both held the world welterweight championship. They hated each other and Basilio, a man without fear, fought with a crude insistence of Rocky Marciano. They signed for a second fight at Chicago Stadium, on March 25, 1958. Robinson was then 37 by his own account, 38 by the record books and 39 by the reckoning of some managers. By any calculation he was old as fighters go.

Covering my first big fight in America, (though I had earlier reported Virgil Atkins *v.* Isaac Logart at Madison Square Garden), perhaps magnified the importance of the occasion for me. The fighters belonged to a different league from those I had seen in Britain. Robinson, who seldom belittled opponents, reckoned Basilio had more talent for onion farming than fighting and fancied he'd win by a k.o. 'I should have knocked him out last time but I caught him too near the end of the rounds.' I recall Sugar saying. A bystander quipped, 'It wouldn't be too late if you started earlier.' It was Joe Louis, hired by the promotion to root for Robinson.

Anxious reporters filled three rows around a scarlet roped ring that had 100 lamps drenching white light on the gladiators. We took off our coats although outside the temperature hovered on freezing point. In a snap poll of the 34

ringside writers (including that gentleman of boxing litera-
ture, the late George Whiting of the London *Evening
Standard*) twenty-one tipped Basilio.

I had little attention to spare for speculation. This was a
very big occasion for me and my hands were clamming at
the thought of writing for a deadline. When the publicity
pedlars piped down, the police took up stance outside the
dressing rooms and the familiar old timers were paraded in
the ring. Robinson and Basilio scowled at each other as
sealed gloves were issued.

Robinson's hair had been carefully marcelled but within
sixty seconds it was in disarray in the most fiercesome first
round I have ever seen in boxing. Basilio butted, elbowed
and palmed. Robinson looked appealingly at short, silver
haired referee, Frank Sikora. He merely waved play on.
Sugar retaliated and added rabbit blows for good measure.
They were still fighting deliberately, furiously, after the first
round bell went and had to be prised apart. One of
Robinson's seconds, Honey Brewer, climbed into Basilio's
corner presumably to watch for hidden horseshoes in the
gloves or forbidden stimulants but he was wrestled away by
tubby, Joe Netro, Basilio's tough manager.

Such Shenanigans in Britain would have caused Board
of Control officials to throw a fit, but in Chicago, in those
days at least, – the rule books were parked at the gate.
Robinson and Basilio were each collecting 260,000 dollars!
'For that kind of money,' said a ringsider, 'leave the two
bums to fight it out.'

For a further fourteen rounds of legalised mayhem, (though
much of the rough stuff had been abandoned for mutual
respect), the fight see-sawed and Basilio's left eye blew up to
look like an ugly, purple plum. Both tried to seek respite by
clinging to the ropes – and to each other.

It was a fight that injection-moulded itself into one's
memory, an event hardly to be related at all to the timid.
What was the verdict to be? The tension thermometer

climbed unbearably as points were gathered. Battered Basilio knelt, crossed himself and prayed. Robinson stamped his feet impatiently in the rein while anxious acolytes wiped the sacrificed blood from their High Priest's face.

I had scored Robinson a winner but referee Sikora voted against him with 66 to 68 marks. Basilio began to smile. Then the judges saved Sugar. John Bray totalled 71 to 64 for Robinson and Spike McAdams gave his casting vote at 72 to 65, Robinson reached for his middleweight crown for the fifth time.

Sugar Ray was too exhausted to talk and Basilio, as Robinson had predicted, went to hospital for facial repairs. 20,000 fans who had paid 351,955 dollars (£125,200) went home satisfied.

I finished my despatch before they had dismantled the ring and within hours the *Evening News* headline 'Sugar Canes Him' was being quoted throughout America. It was an occasion that gave Robinson, and me, great satisfaction.

The Sugar Ray saga sometimes seems larger than life. He was born, in Detroit, and lived in the 'black bottom' district. Black was the family colour and bottom is where they were at. In 1932 his parents were divorced and his mother, who worked at a laundry, took him and his sisters, Marie and Evelyn, to New York.

The only thing phoney about Robinson was his name. He was born Walker Smith – he's still Smitty to his oldest friends – but the controllers of boxing forced the change of name. He might well have become Charlie Suggins or Joe Blow but luckily he chanced on the catchy name of a pal who now runs a Harlem bar, a man who really has the right to call his place 'Ray Robinson's.

Little, weedy Smith, scaling 8 st., had been caught crap-shooting on a sidewalk. Others scarpered when the local cops appeared, but even at 14, the Sugar-to-be had the scent for money. He was scooping up the nickles and pennies (top stakes) when the arm of the law descended. The cop convinced the Harlem newcomer that he should put his youthful efforts into something more productive and a kid named Warren Jones, took scruffy Smitty to the 129th Street athletic club, Salem Crescent, which was run by Warren's uncle, George Gainford.

The meeting developed into one of boxing's longest and most successful partnerships. Gainford, nicknamed The Emperor, was Sugar's manager, (for the record), but whether Gainford managed Ray or Ray managed Gainford is a matter on which of the pair have been known to disagree. Together they made a fortune.

Only when Robinson commented on the partnership in his autobiography *Sugar Ray* (Putman), a book skilfully scripted by New York Times columnist, Dave Anderson, did the old-time partnership show signs of strain.

But the initial tutoring of Gainford, and the later attentions of the roly-poly Harry Wiley, fashioned Sugar into a world beater. They tied skinny Smitty's right hand to his side and taught him to box with the left. Robinson's left jab, and the way he switched a potential straight punch to a hook, was superb.

Being able to deliver blows at flashing speed was Robinson's forte. I recall him demonstrating how the blow – or, in my case, the single finger prod – could hurt if it caught you by surprise. He made me watch him push a forefinger into my ribs. Naturally, it did not hurt. 'Now turn your eyes away,' he said. He then jabbed a finger into my stomach. The shock made it comparatively hurtful. 'That's the way I planned to catch an opponent,' he said. 'I was never a strong guy. I was probably the weakest middleweight of them all. But catch a guy by surprise and he'll go.'

Sugar Ray a weakling? He could have fooled me. Having learned the rudiments of the ring, at 15, the impetuous kid was ready for public fights. The prizes he could swap for cash would be handy. But New York State forbids boxing under 16, so Smitty grabbed the identity card of a clubmate,

Ray Robinson, who was 17. The great name was launched. Gainford, with an eye for publicity, added the tag Sugar because Smitty's boxing was so sweet.

The real Robinson never made the big league but the takeover Ray became Golden Gloves featherweight champion in 1939, and lightweight champion in 1940.

Around the Bronx there was a brawling knock-out puncher much feared by the New York amateurs. It was decided to use him as a test of Sugar's strength and temperament. They figured Sugar would lose, but the experience would be good for him. Little Smitty, after all, was going on 18 according to his assumed registration. The fact that he was just turned 16 had not occurred to the matchmakers. Gainford dutifully warned his kid of the punching prowess of the opponent. 'Stay out of trouble, jab and move, and let's see if this guy runs out of gas,' said Gainford. But that was not the way Sugar Ray had planned to fight. 'You mean I've got to get him before he gets me?' asked Ray. He knocked out the Bronx tough guy with the first punch of the fight. They knew for sure that the new Ray Robinson was destined to become a great one.

There was also another character who liked the name 'Sugar Ray' and insisted on his right to use it. Smitty suggested it would be a good idea if he forgot it. The character, who must have been foolish as well as stubborn said 'no'. Smitty took him on and smashed him in the first round. The name claimant was still not satisfied. So Ray did it again!

Robinson went seven years as amateur and pro without losing until he conceded 17 lb. against the rough Jake La Motta. He reversed that loss four times – who else but Robinson would tangle five times with the Bronx Bull? – and was not beaten again until the shock against Turpin.

On the same night when a rising Robinson k.o.'d Joe Echevarria, the great Henry Armstrong lost the world welterweight title to the ringwise Fritzie Zivic. Robinson was to beat both of them.

In 1947 Jimmy Doyle, a capable boxer, died after losing to Robinson. Some say the death deeply affected Ray's career. But he knew the risks of the ring and learned to live with the tragedy. He gave money away like it was going out of style. In 1950 he fought Charley Fusari for one dollar, giving 33,000 dollars to the Damon Runyon Cancer Research Fund.

The kid who had shined shoes, danced for dimes and swiped food from supermarkets, used his unique talents and old-fashioned guts to make it big. In his heyday he drove a fuchsia Cadillac convertible and frittered away £250 a night on hand outs. But when the end came he found that many of his friends and flatterers had vanished like the dollars he had dispensed so lavishly.

Tax involvement, property deals, and the marital problems which Sugar Ray seemed to attract, completed the syndrome : big money, big spending, big talk – and big fall.

The ring end came at Pittsburgh, November 10, 1965. He lost a ten rounds decision against Joey Archer, who was not a second rater but was still not considered in Robinson's class.

'You still think you have it, but you suddenly find out you have not,' Ray told me. He left the ring that night to the cheers of sympathy. They were small consolation to the proud man who had won 175 times. 'When a boxer like Archer could push me over with a tap on the head I knew I'd gone,' he said.

The official retirement came at a party a month later. Two years afterwards *Ring* magazine elected him to Boxing's Hall of Fame. Madison Square Garden, then the mecca of the sport, honoured Robinson as the greatest boxer of all time. Many of Robinson's victims, including Turpin, were there to shake his hand and agree with the honour.

He stood in the ring, still with sleek hips, a pencil thin moustache, high cheekbones, looking like a carbon copy of Clark Gable. He beamed with an almost girlish pleasure at being admired.

The life of retirement was, in many ways, tougher for

Robinson than the rigours of training and fighting had been. As his 50th birthday loomed he was still going. 'I guess the batteries haven't run down,' – he'd say.

Times were not as good for Robinson – despite the fact of outpointing Uncle Sam's internal revenue for one bout – and he turned, inevitably, to acting and cabaret. When Sugar Ray walks into a room he still creates sweet vibrations. For example there was hardly a dry eye in the place when they honoured him at the Anglo American Sporting Club in London in 1969. 'For his unprecedented contribution to boxing,' they said.

The end has not been the way Sugar Ray would have wanted it but he accepted it without rancour and without regret. 'If I had the chance I'd do it all over again,' he says.

There can never be another like him.

(Some of the Sugar Ray charisma is being imparted into others. His current job is the figurehead of the US Government backed Youth Foundation. As always, Sugar is doing his thing in style. It's a job for life – and he loves it.)

4

Jack Dempsey

Jack Dempsey offered a warm but expensive welcome to the world that walked along Broadway, New York, where a 3 ft. red neon blazed the old champ's name above a restaurant. 'If I hadn't knocked out Jess Willard and been heavyweight champion of the world, I would probably have been sweeping this joint out instead of half owning it,' said Dempsey.

It is sixty years since Dempsey officially became a pro fighter – losing his first recorded contest on points! – and forty-eight years since he lost the world championship to Gene Tunney. Yet Dempsey, despite an arthritic hip that now restricts his activities, starred in the longest-running show on Broadway. People flocked to see him.

Jack lives with his half-Italian fourth wife, Deanna, at an apartment in nearby East 53rd Street, Manhattan, where he hates having to take life easy after a lifetime of roaming. 'My batteries haven't worn down yet, but the damn hip stops me getting about like I used to.' Jack recently confided to me. 'And you know something else,' he said, 'I've got to the stage where it is hard for me to remember people's names and even a lot of the guys I fought. Its so damn annoying.'

Dempsey still thinks of himself as the marvellously athletic-looking champ instead of having reached his 79th birthday in 1974.

There was still plenty of fight left in the great one when I saw him last year (1974). He and long-time business partner,

Jack Amiel, had successfully defeated the New York property speculators who had booked the restaurant site for demolition. The changing face of Manhattan has severely hit the restaurant trade, but that wide-eyed section of tourists known to the inhabitants as the Sunday suckers streamed into Dempsey's bar.

There were tiled portico representations of the young, handsome Dempsey in a fighting mood and the star of the place smothered customers with the warmth of his 'Hiya, feller' welcome that looks like a ponderous bear hoping to be fed buns. It was a pride blow to Dempsey when the building was condemned in 1975. The famous bar has closed.

Dempsey is hero-worshipped beyond belief. He personifies the inner feelings of every man with a red rawness and ruggedness. And yet Dempsey is the most courteous and considerate fighter I have ever known. He was once the most powerful, ruthless and dangerous unarmed man in the world, yet he remains so humble and suffers fools gladly.

I have seen visitors to his restaurant plead with Jack to knock them out for the privilege of being able to boast that the great Dempsey had flattened them. 'I'd give guys a friendly clip on the chin that buckled their knees and they would go home happy,' Jack said, 'But I'm getting to be an old guy myself now and, hell, supposing I couldn't knock another old guy out? I'd never live it down.'

It is a gratifying experience to be in Dempsey's company and it was particularly satisfying to have chaired a recent private function honouring Dempsey at the London Sportsman Club given by the Boxing Writers' Club. Our tribute was spontaneous and I swear tears welled in Jack's eyes when he realised that his audience were all hardened scribes who had paid to pay homage.

'Sportswriters around the world have kept me alive,' he said, 'I'm very grateful to them.'

Listening to Dempsey's modesty made me cringe at the thought of other so-called sportsmen, often petulant to both public and press, who are not big enough to shine Dempsey's shoes either as a competitor or person.

Yet the brutal facts, that Dempsey does not deny, are that he was the most *un*popular heavyweight of all time when he reigned as world champion from 1919 until 1926. He was accused of being a slacker, a draft dodger, a cheesecake champion and Hollywood champion.

Dempsey fought only five times in the seven years and one month that he held the title. It was two defeats by Gene Tunney that finally turned Dempsey into a hero and legend.

It was Dempsey, without any doubt, who transformed boxing from semi-shamble promotions to a highly commercialised profession.

Had Dempsey been fighting with today's added rewards of world-wide TV he must have become a dollar billionaire.

Dempsey's fight with Georges Carpentier in New Jersey, 1921, was the first million dollar gate – 1,626,580 dollars to be exact. Federal and state tax deducted 292,978.66. (How did they deduce the sixty-six cents?)

Dempsey's second famous clash with Gene Tunney at Soldier's Field, Chicago, 1927, is still the only fight to attract more than two million dollars for the 'live' gate. The proceeds from a 104,943 attendance was 2,658,660 dollars.

Dempsey, born William Harrison and nicknamed Jack by his elder brother, Bernie, was tagged 'The Manassa Mauler' by Damon Runyon because W.H. was born at Manassa, Colorado. He was the ninth child, born June 24, 1895, of a Mormon father, Hyrum, who lived to the age of 95.

Dempsey's mother was Cecilia Smoot ('the most magnificent human being I ever knew,' said Jack) and both parents had Indian blood. Jack considers himself basically Irish, with Cherokee strain, plus a splash of Jewish from his great-great-grandmother.

Jack's Indian strain was evident with his black hair, high cheek bones and a quick, pigeon-toed glide. Much of his

Western accent has disappeared but when he arrived in New York his talk was not like the accepted Western sheriff. His voice was so high that, according to Jack, 'the bullies agreed to fight me because I sounded like a girl'.

Tradition has it that Dempsey learned to fight because it was the natural result of poverty and the rough, outback life on the last American frontier. He was always a restless hustler who came swinging out of the Wild West and made a dollar any way he could.

But tradition, like many other repeated boxing stories, is wrong. Jack was a good miner who enjoyed digging for coal, gold and even uranium. He was also a good cowboy. He could have made a comfortable living at either vocation.

But Jack Dempsey dreamed only of being a prize fighter. It had little to do with hunger. It was the way of life that attracted him and when Jack became world champion, thirteen years after first believing he was born to fight, it did not surprise him.

Only the cold reception upset him. People would jeer on sidewalks, call 'slacker' from passing cars, from windows, but nobody ever said it to Dempsey's face. A San Francisco sportswriter began the World War One charge against Dempsey and the public took up the cry.

Yet Dempsey had not broken the Draft Act and the draft board had considered him entitled to deferment because he supported a wife, Maxine, a piano player later to confess being a prostitute, from Walla Walla, Washington. Their marriage lasted less than a year, but it was the oath Maxine took in a San Francisco court that wrecked Dempsey's reputation.

The first Mrs Dempsey alleged that Jack did not support her and the allegation was interpreted as a falsifying of draft papers. His trial for defrauding the government lasted five days, but the jury took only fifteen minutes to return a verdict of 'Not Guilty'.

There was also the most publicised picture incident of

Dempsey's career that swayed the nation against him. A government official asked Dempsey to pose for a photograph intended to encourage more men to work in shipyards. It was at the Sun shipyard, near Philadelphia, only months before the 1918 armistice in France.

Dempsey was the easy-going man eager to oblige the war effort. He donned striped overalls and held a drill, while shaking hands with the government official. 'It was the stupidest picture ever taken,' sighs Dempsey today. The newspapers published full length photos showing Dempsey wearing patent leather shoes while supposedly working. He never expected the people to believe he was a regular shipyard worker. He was villified for the intended goodwill gesture.

Dempsey did not make a similar mistake for the action replay twenty-four years later. When the bell struck for America's entry into World War Two Dempsey was 47, but he walked into the Whitehall Building at the tip of Manhattan island and asked to enrol into the services. 'This time,' pleaded Dempsey, 'I'm not doing it just for a picture and I don't want people to think it's a big act.'

Within hours pictures were plastered on newspaper front pages of the veteran ex-champion enlisting. And then came the crunch. He was rejected as being too old for the U.S. Army. Dempsey was both sick and angry. 'I'd pleaded with the enrolling Colonel not to take pictures until they were sure I'd been accepted,' said Dempsey.

Some of the early 'slacker' jibes were rewritten. But within a few weeks Dempsey had enlisted with the Coast Guard and became the Lieutenant in charge of fitness at the 15,000-strong base in Brooklyn. He was also the services most wanted man to launch bond rally shows.

Inevitably, the public relation brains wanted Dempsey to pose for a propaganda picture and they dreamt up the idea of taking Dempsey to Okinawa when the heavy fighting had ceased and the Marine Corps were engaged in mopping-up operations. The Coast Guard wanted 'proof' of their involvement in the hand-to-hand battling.

Lieutenant Dempsey went Jap hunting as instructed with a snap-happy photographer in attendance. Having squirted a flame thrower to weed out Jap soldiers, Dempsey saw a prey running from hiding and he was able to grab his prisoner by the neck. It took Dempsey time to get the squirming Jap under control while the photographer yelled, 'Turn him towards us, Commander'. But when the cameraman saw the face of the Jap he burst out laughing. 'Sir,' he said, 'That battling Jap is ninety years old!'

Dempsey checked and smiled, 'He looks at least seventy.' That was the end of Dempsey's attempts to please for a picture.

At the end of the war the ex-champion was awarded four ribbons and a Legion of Merit and was asked to stay as a regular Coast Guard officer. He declined, but the record had been put straight.

Though Dempsey's upbringing was shrouded with poverty his parents came from well-to-do families who owned land and a grocery store. His grandfather was a sheriff and county surveyor. His mother never weighed more than a flyweight, but his father was 6 ft. 1 in., though weighing no more than eleven stones.

Jack's affection for his mother was lasting. He tells the story of her final hours in 1943. 'Are you feeling any better, Sister Dempsey,' asked a Mormon doctor. 'You know very well that I'm dying. If you ask me how I feel again I'll get out of this bed and punch you on the nose,' she replied.

Jack says his mother died on that note of common sense and courage. He believed she was approaching the age of ninety.

The Dempsey clan, which grew to eleven, moved from West Virginia to the Mormon-founded frontier town of Manassa around 1880. The population was then 100. Two of Jack's brothers died young, one by his own hand, a third was stabbed in the back while selling papers in Salt Lake City. A sister also died before Jack was four.

Dempsey barely remembers the town of Manassa but he remembers never being really hungry. The Mormon faith saw to that. He also remembers having to extract his own teeth and the family not being able to afford a doctor.

It took two years for a seven-year-old Jack (his mother called him Harry) to reach Uncompahgre, Colorado, on the family prairie schooner. It was about 600 miles from Manassa. Crossing the great divide two of the family horses died.

Young Jack worked at everything from digging to dish washing, peddling magazines, and fighting in saloons to collect the dimes for the last kid standing. 'When I was on my way up,' said Jack in his autobiography *Massacre in the Sun* (Heinemann), 'many people said I was a bum. If being uneducated, owning a ragged shirt and a pair of patched pants, and having holes in your shoes make a man a bum, I was a bum.'

Dempsey yearned to be a fighter and to strengthen his chin he chewed gum from pine trees and pickled his face and hands in beef brine to make it as tough as leather. He began as a greenhorn, poor fighter, calling himself Kid Blackie, who could be hit easily. But Jack was a natural hard hitter.

He grew into a perfectly proportioned heavyweight, though comparatively slight when compared to the modern jumbo sizes of Muhammad Ali, George Foreman, or even Joe Frazier. Dempsey stood just over 6 ft., though his natural style was crouching, and weighed 190 lb., (13 st. 8 lb.), roughly the same as Henry Cooper. He would have been dwarfed by Foreman or Ali, though he was bigger than Floyd Patterson.

But Dempsey's greatness, apart from the power of his punches, was his ability to crush much heavier opposition with the sheer viciousness of his attacks.

Jack Dempsey

Jack (Doc) Kearns, who became Dempsey's manager for the best part of his career – a rightly successful yet perpetually feuding partnership – extolled the viciousness of his protégé's punch. By the end of Dempsey's career, when he had attained an idolatry and public love that had transcended anything ever known in the world of sport, nine million dollars had been paid to watch him fight.

Kearns, whom I knew in recent years, was the greatest managerial schemer of all time and he wanted to write a book entitled *Larceny for a Living – I Love it!* His nefarious machinations over the years were seldom hindered by scruples, though among the fraternity he was adored as a high liver and big spender.

Kearns handled a least five million dollars for Dempsey and never gave Jack an account in writing!

It was Kearns's liberal slicing of expenses 'off the top' before he took what seems to me a ludicrous slice of fifty per cent of Dempsey's fight purses that caused constant bickering between boxer and manager. They were offered a small fortune, during the sixties, for permission to film an accurate account of their working lives. It might have been a Hollywood big hit. But old Kearns (he also managed Archie Moore and Joey Maxim) still wanted his complete half share. The deal was never signed and the Doc died, aged 80 upwards, in 1963.

It was a pity that Kearns, in an article published posthumously, claimed that when Dempsey won the heavyweight title in three torrid rounds from the giant Jess Willard on July 4, 1919, Jack's hands had been wrapped in bandages soaked in plaster of Paris.

Dempsey was, understandably, angry and vehemently denied Kearns's allegation, eventually suing the publisher of the article.

Willard, the biggest man ever to hold the title, lived to the ripe age of 87, and claimed that Kearns had confirmed what he had known all along. He would never become friendly with Dempsey, even when Jack made efforts of handshakes and financial help. Willard believed he had been pummelled to ribbons by a rampaging fighter holding bolts in his hands!

Willard, at 6 ft. $6\frac{1}{4}$ in., weighing $17\frac{1}{2}$ st., officially outweighed Dempsey by 4 st. 4 lb., but Jack has always contended that he weighed 180 lb, and not the 182 or 184 that continued to be listed in boxing history books. By any account the weight difference was great.

Willard was 6–5 favourite to keep his title and many believed the slight Dempsey would melt in the 100 degree heat at Toledo, Ohio. Instead, Dempsey massacred the giant, splintering Willard's cheek with the first punch landed and Dempsey flung himself at the towering man like an infuriated animal. Willard was put down seven times in the first round, though Jack only recalls four counts, and poor Willard, who had become the nation's idol by taking the championship from Jack Johnson, finished the round with a battered, bleeding face and staring aimlessly into space as he groped around the canvas.

Willard's seconds – they really needed a crane – managed to haul the giant to his corner while pandemonium reigned. Referee Ollie Pecord (or Picard) had raised Dempsey's hand in victory and Kearns was said to have taken a bet of 10,000 dollars, at the odds of 10–1, that Dempsey would win in the first round.

Hence Kearns's 1964 allegation that he had 'doctored' Dempsey's bandages. But there was more confusion to come. Nobody had heard the bell ending the first round and Kearns had sent Dempsey scurrying out of the ring and heading for his dressing-room. Again the most reliable historians have repeated the 'silent bell' tale.

In fact, there never was a first round bell! The workers at the stadium specially built for 20,000 – the heat boiled the resin out of the back benches! – had laced the ring canvas so clumsily that they covered the bell, which put the very necessary instrument out of commission. Timekeeper,

Warren Barbour, later to become a New Jersey senator, was issued with a police whistle instead. It became the whistle-stop championship.

When Barbour made it known that he had ended the first round, by whistling and gesturing, during the referee's last count, Kearns hastily recalled the confused Dempsey from the milling crowd. The film of the fight shows an excited white-capped Kearns flinging his arms around as he beckons Dempsey, with a towel around his shoulders, back into action.

Nobody could have objected if the U.S. Government had outlawed boxing, in any form, after what followed in the Dempsey-Willard disgrace. The big man should never have been allowed to come off his stool. In three minutes he had been punished more than any other champion. He was to be pitied and boxing ceased to become a sport when somebody, presumably the referee, allowed Willard to continue for two more complete rounds.

Willard, with two front teeth missing, a cheek later found to be splintered in thirteen pieces, finally collapsed on his stool when his chief second, Ike O'Neill, finally threw in the towel – about six minutes overdue.

Dempsey, of course, could not be blamed though he may have warranted criticism for failing to put Willard away at the start of the second round. But for nine minutes Dempsey lambasted the bruised and blood-stained wreck before him. Willard had displayed a previously unsuspected and super-human form of bravery to occasionally hit back at his tor-mentor.

Dempsey, upon oath, denied having any form of sub-stance hardening on his hands. 'I didn't need plaster and I wouldn't have gotten away with it even if I tried,' he said. Willard had a representative, big Walter Monaghan, standing over Dempsey in his dressing room during the taping of hands and also following him down the aisle to his corner.

In America this practice is still acknowledged and in Britain championship contestants have tape and bandage issued by a Board of Control inspector with each hand officially franked before the boxers enter the ring. No extra cover or the hidden horseshoe can be slipped inside a glove!

Because of the amount of damage Dempsey caused to Willard there is a theory that his hands could have been hardened, but I discount the Kearns allegation of plaster of Paris powder sprinkled on bandages because it would have been too clumsy and easily spotted after the fight. A recent experiment, copying Kearns' procedure showed that the plaster crumbled off the hands and was worthless. The closest to the truth, I suggest, comes from an article by Joe Vila, a boxing authority of his day, from the New York *Evening Sun* of June 30, 1920. It gives extra credence because the article appeared less than a year after the slaughter in the sun.

If Vila seemed to dismiss the meatiest part of his story with a casual reference in the final paragraphs, it was only because it did not appear significant in that era of skulduggery and sharp dealing. In an interview with Dempsey's second, Jimmy DeForest, who had been in Dempsey's corner at Toledo, DeForest discussed the demolition of Willard thus...

'Jack followed my instructions to the letter. I told him after landing half a dozen lefts to cut loose with the right for Willard's heart. The first time Jack drove the right home it was all over. When I handled Kid McCoy I used a certain adhesive tape to bandage his hands. As soon as McCoy drew on the gloves, the tape hardened and, as a result, he was able to inflict unusual punishment. I wound Dempsey's hands with the same kind of bandages, which Willard's people inspected. The story that Jack was supposed to have carried a bolt in his hand or had them covered with aluminum pads is a lie. No doubt his bandages became hardened and that was why he cut Willard's face to ribbons.'

I am grateful to an old friend, Arthur Daley, of the

'Get up, you bum', Ali taunts Liston in their second fight

A badly cut Cooper is about to lose to Ali in their 1966 Title fight

Early 'Ali-style' publicity at its best. *Right:* The Great Brown Bomber – Joe Louis in fighting pose

222. La Boxe — JACK JOHNSON
Champion du Monde   C. M.

Jack Johnson – the first
negro Heavyweight
Champion.
Left: The legendary
Jimmy Wilde

The Rock (Rocky Marciano) demolishes Joe Louis

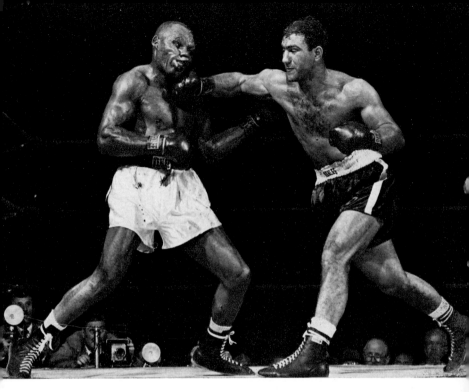

The punch that packs power! Marciano distorts Jersey Joe
Walcott's face

Marciano in retirement chats with the author

Even in his seventies, the fists of Jack Dempsey still look fearsome!

'Toe-to-toe, eye-to-eye'
Sugar Ray Robinson
battles it out with
Carmen Basilio

Archie Moore (on the
right) fights Pompey in
London

New York Times, who passed away during 1974, for this archive information.

Dempsey's record is studded with sensation and knockouts. When he was out of the title picture in 1927 Dempsey won 53 successive fights by a k.o., all but four of them were either in the first or second round. He finished seriously in 1932 and embarked on a career of refereeing both boxing and wrestling which brought his final comeback with three bouts in 1940 at the age of 45.

These bouts were 'sham' and promoted when a wrestler would question referee Dempsey's decision and then be challenged to a return 'for real' with gloves on. But even in his forties Dempsey did not know how to 'carry' an opponent and a character called Cowboy Luttrell was left-hooked out of the ring and carted off to hospital.

At the height of his career Dempsey was asked to 'carry' George Carpentier by promoter Tex Rickard. I doubt if any fight except, perhaps, the return between Joe Louis and Max Schmeling, ever had such a build-up as the first million dollar gate at Boyle's Thirty Acre Oval, New Jersey. It was also probably the worst mismatch for the heavyweight championship until Pete Rademacher challenged Floyd Patterson for the championship in his first professional fight.

Dempsey, so refreshingly honest, also agrees that the fight with Carpentier was among his easiest. Even before the fight he considered Carpentier 'an easy touch'.

With Dempsey busy fighting in courts and fighting off the slackers slurs, Carpentier the handsome French soldier, was hailed like a hero as if he had won the War single handed. But with his good looks and fine physique Carpentier was not a genuine heavyweight. He was too slight to be in the same town as Dempsey, let alone the same ring.

Dempsey, through Kearns, took 300,000 dollars and waived the option of 50 per cent of the gate. His decision robbed him of 150,000 dollars. But neither Dempsey nor Kearns, despite the publicity for the fight, believed it would be the biggest money taker of all. They knew it would be one-sided.

Because the chief of police feared the scaffold erected arena might fall down, the fight was started at 3 p.m. Promoter Rickard, who must have been the smartest of them all, was overcome by the attendance of high society. He crammed 91,000 people into his makeshift arena.

'Jack, this is the biggest day the boxing business ever had,' said Rickard, 'I don't want you messing it up. Don't kill him, Jack. If you kill him you kill boxing.'

It was suggested at the time that Dempsey was set to 'carry' Carpentier for a few rounds to be sure of some film footage. But Dempsey still remembers what he said to Rickard only minutes before the fight. 'Tex,' he said, 'Tell that Frog not to run and I'll give you a good fight. But this guy is going out as soon as I can take him. I'm not carrying nobody for nobody, even for you.'

The arena, a writer said, looked like a saucer of honey filled with flies. Dempsey was again hurt by his reception. He was still cast as a villain. It was not a particularly good fight. The first round was merely a feeler, with Carpentier looking as though fear were thrashed inside him. The Frenchman did land his feared right in the second but it was too high on Dempsey's face to be effective.

When Carpentier sensed that his best punch could not check the ferocious Dempsey he was more concerned with survival than bent on winning. By round four Dempsey had learned to duck inside Carpentier's leads and though the Frenchman bounced five successive punches off Dempsey's head it was Dempsey's final counter, a left hook, that put Carpentier down for a nine count.

He got up and stumbled like a learner into Dempsey, trying to hold and nullify Dempsey's next attack. But the champion had too much animal instinct to tolerate such crudity. He cracked home another left, and as Carpentier was falling, sent a following right to the body. Georges groped on the canvas, rolled over, and made a futile effort to beat the count. It was all over in 57 seconds of round four.

Surprisingly, the press did not hail Dempsey but praised Carpentier's courage – such as it was. The champion felt bitter. 'I was just the butcher who happened to win,' he shrugged.

In 1927 Dempsey met Jack Sharkey. At the time Dempsey had been dethroned, while Sharkey was later to become the only man to win the heavyweight championship on a foul, against Max Schmeling. Dempsey destroyed Sharkey in seven rounds.

Sharkey (now a fly-fishing champion) also fought Joe Louis. His comparison of them is fascinating. He says, 'The beating I got from Dempsey was worth 251,000 dollars; the one I got from Louis was worth only 58,000 dollars. Louis was the cleanest fighter I ever met. He knocked me down nine times, waited for me to get up, and asked 'You all right?' But Dempsey would hit you anytime, anywhere. If you put them both in a telephone booth to settle the issue the guy who would emerge would be Dempsey.'

Dempsey was all feline, either a wildcat or tiger. He did not observe the niceties of the Marquis of Queensberry rules. Never was Dempsey's ferocity better exemplified than against Luis Angel Firpo, the Argentinian they tagged the Wild Bull of the Pampas.

The fight took place at New York's Polo Grounds, 1923, and it lasted only three minutes and 57 seconds. But it was the lustiest quick big-fight of the lot, and, of course, it was another million dollar special for Dempsey which says a great deal for a man who was supposed to have been hated. He was involved in five over-a-million dollar gate fights, compared with Louis's three.

(Not all of Dempsey's historic fights were promotional winners. The biggest fiasco in history involved Dempsey against Tom Gibbons at the little cow-town of Shelby,

Montana, whose inhabitants were foolish enough to guarantee 300,000 dollars to Dempsey. The whole episode sounds like fiction. Joe Benjamim, the last survivor with Dempsey of that 1923 title fight, told me that Doc Kearns broke the banks of the town to get the cash and he stuffed the money in a mail bag to ride out of town while the unfortunate backers were debating whether or not to lynch him.

The fight was poor and harmed Dempsey's reputation for instant destruction. Gibbons fought for 7,500 dollars, but received nothing, not even training expenses. Dempsey, with a referee handpicked by Kearns, received a 15-round decision.)

Firpo weighed 15 st. 6 lb., stood 6 ft. 3 in., and was strong enough to poleaxe a bull with his fists. And before the fight was five-seconds old the 82,000 crowd were on their feet – and Dempsey was on his back. The champion had lunged and missed with a left-hook and Firpo landed a countering right. Dempsey the durable went down, but he clambered up before a count began and with emotions raw and primitive Dempsey rushed in to finish the job. They exchanged body blows at a furious rate and Firpo began going up and down like a yo-yo. Each time Firpo went down Dempsey stood within punching range, showing no mercy, because at that time a clean, step back break was not needed.

But the battered brute emerged from the same primordial ooze and swung back at the on-rushing Dempsey who reeled back across the ring as though having been flung from a catapult. Dempsey fell backwards over the middle rope and clean out of the ring. The Associated Press photo of Dempsey disappearing with feet high in the air is among the most published in boxing history.

Dempsey crashed on the typewriter of reporter Jack Lawrence who propped Dempsey up and helped shove the champion back into the fray. When Dempsey scrambled back into the ring, his hip aching, he was only one second away from being dethroned.

Dempsey fell into a clinch and awaited the reprieve of the bell. Strictly speaking journalists were not supposed to heave Dempsey back into the ring but if, like me, you have ever had a heavyweight thrown in your lap you will find it difficult to bother about rules.

Firpo, having muffed the greatest chance of his life, was suddenly shocked into immobility, and Dempsey showed his greatness by clubbing a right clean on Firpo's jaw, delivered with crushing force, and no back answers. Big Luis was knocked out by the perfect punch in 57 seconds of the second round. Without realising it Dempsey was really knocked off the golden pedestal by crude Firpo because he was to lose a year later to Gene Tunney.

Tunney, the war hero, was an under-rated heavy with a fine style and the ability to absorb a hard punch. Only the windmill hitter, Harry Greb, had beaten Tunney, but Tunney had the best of all four subsequent fights against Greb. His upright style and skill was ideally suited to cope with a 31-year-old Dempsey who had not fought for just over twelve months and was engaged in legal squabbles with his second wife, actress Estelle Taylor. Dempsey suffered from his inactivity. He had gone soft.

Tunney has told us many times that he kept Dempsey 'in a test-tube' for a year, studying his every move and rehearsing to both out-think and out-punch him.

Dempsey's seven year grip of sport's richest prize was broken by the Shakespeare quoting friend of George Bernard Shaw. Tunney's points victory at Philadelphia in 1926 – Dempsey's only fight that year – also explodes a present day myth that the old timers fought to a finish over marathon courses. In fact, both the Dempsey-Tunney fights were mere ten rounders but recognised as official title matches.

Defeat for Dempsey showed his decline as a fighter (or could Tunney have beaten Dempsey at peak?) and his overnight rise as a hero. It was Tunney who became unpopular for destroying the invincible legend. The public yearned for a return – as though Rickard had not already plotted a second helping. (Rickard, incidentally, was rated so highly as promoter that when he died his body lay in state at Madison Square Garden.)

Exactly a year later the return fight took place in Chicago and became the famous battle of the Long Count. In the seventh round Dempsey floored Tunney for ringsider timings of fourteen seconds. Referee Dave Barry was insistent that Dempsey retire to a neutral corner – a regulation introduced for this occasion – before he took up the count. Tunney propped his right fist on a rope and waited until the dispute was sorted out.

Dempsey has never been adamant that Tunney could not have beaten a regulation ten count, but he was angry that the referee lacked consistency.

The Long Count round has been debated in practically every saloon and sports column in the world since that memorable night, yet few ever bother to recall what happened in the ninth round. Tunney knocked Dempsey down and the referee made a big show of shoving Tunney to a neutral corner and then rushing back to take up the timekeeper's count of 'seven' over Dempsey.

When Tunney was down the referee argued loud and long with Dempsey and began his count from one, instead of the seven the knockdown timekeeper had tolled. Hence Tunney's longer respite.

Tunney, who became a highly respected businessman, (he's now healthy, though almost completely deaf) has laughingly said, 'I only stayed down because Jack looked tired and needed the rest.' Tunney gave Rickard a cheque for 9,554.46 dollars, the balance of his 990,445.54 dollars purse, because Tunney wanted to frame a cheque for one million dollars. Dempsey's 'short end' of the purse was 425,000 dollars, the highest for a non-champion until Muhammad Ali came along in the inflationary seventies.

'I guess everything turned out for the best,' says Dempsey

today. 'The people grew to like me. People have been so kind. I'm not sure that I even deserve it. But I'm damn grateful.'

Outside of his ring business hours Dempsey never hurt a soul. In his own words, he was a sucker with his money. But he has never wanted. There are millions of Americans and admirers all over the world who still regard Jack Dempsey as 'the champ', the perfect fighting man.

(Dempsey's official record was 69 fights, k.o.'d 47, won seven on points; one by foul, five no-decision, lost four on points and one by k.o.)

5
Jack Johnson

The most controversial heavyweight of them all : that was
Jack Johnson. Some authorities, including ring historian Nat
Fleischer, have rated him the No. 1 of all time. I don't
support that view though Johnson was, unquestionably, the
greatest of his era.

Perhaps his most outstanding attribute was the ring cunning that made him the despair of so many opponents – and
made him despised at the same time.

His rise to world heavyweight supremacy took place against
a background of white envy and jealousy in 1908.

From a likeable young man, (born in Galveston, Texas,
March 31, 1878), with little more than a set of gold teeth
to distinguish him from most other negroes, Johnson acquired
a very dubious image justified, perhaps, by the way he
blazed a trail of noisy arrogance across the world. He had
beaten up Jim Jeffries in a Reno débâcle, fallen foul of
U.S. Federal Laws and fled to Europe.

We have come to regard Muhammad Ali as an extrovert
among extroverts, but Muhammad at his most crass is like a
choir boy beside Johnson who preferred to be called 'L'il
Arthur' – his real name.

Johnson had experience in many fields outside the prize
ring. He had been a house painter, a docker, a coral fisher,
a groom, a clerk, a musician, a bullfighter, a volunteer secret
agent for the U.S. Government, and possibly also for the
Kaiser, a nightclub owner, a wrestler, a preacher, a P.T.

instructor, actor, beer salesman, political orator and patron of the arts.

He was also the only negro ever to deliver an address on the golden rule before a klavern of the Ku Klux Klan. He was matched with a kangaroo and a boa constrictor and legend has it in another strange contest of strength with Grigori Rasputin, the notorious monk at the court of Nicholas II.

His career was highly unusual but Johnson lived an even more remarkable fantasy life which he often failed to distinguish from reality. Writer Finis Farr, for example, is convinced that Johnson firmly believed that a Zeppelin raiding London during World War One was actually following his car, the airship pilot keeping Johnson spotted in a spyglass.

The life of L'il Arthur has held a strange fascination for me since my grandfather told me some of the legends. Grandad knew how to use his fists and became a fixture of the original National Sporting Club.

Grandad hitch-hiked to Plymouth in 1908 to gaze in awe at Johnson against Ben Taylor, the Woolwich terror. Johnson had also fought Al McNamara at Plymouth – his only appearances, other than stage shows, in Britain.

My grandfather had also been friend and masseur to Victor McLaglen, who later became internationally famous as a film actor. McLaglen fought Johnson at Vancouver in 1909.

The Johnsonian saga was so deeply embedded in me that when fight reporting at Houston, Texas, I made a solo journey to Galveston, a 28-mile island, for no other reason than to be able to say that I had been to the birthplace of John Arthur, son of a school janitor, who became Jack Johnson.

His uninhibited personal life made Johnson an object of moral censure. He was always ready to plunge into a brawl and on one occasion had to pay £1,075 damages to a London theatrical manager, Jack Dumaurier, for injuries inflicted. Deplorable as his temperament was, Johnson's free use of his fists appeared less of a transgression against the standards of the day than his sin against the unwritten moral code of Edwardian times. Johnson married a white woman! In fact he married three white women. Only the wife of his early youth was of his own race.

When he was sentenced to one year and one day under the Mann Act for abducting Belle Schreiber across a State line for immoral purposes, Johnson fled the country.

His arrival in London brought many music hall bookings and the champion did his best to provide a cheerful note during the early World War One years. He added a vivid sartorial decoration to the London scene.

He strode down Piccadilly sporting a golden trilby and crocodile skin shoes. His white Benz touring car was upholstered with leopard skin. Under the influence of drink however, Johnson tended to make pro-German remarks and the tide of sympathy quickly turned against him. His London flat was burgled, though little was taken.

He was served with a notice to leave Britain 'within 24 hours' and though American-born Sir Hiram Maxim, inventor of the machine gun, and Lord Lonsdale, a great patron of sport, appealed on Johnson's behalf, the champion decided when a gang of rowdies attacked him that it was wiser to run away and fight another day.

It was at the Savoy Hotel, London, that Johnson agreed to defend his championship against the giant, Jess Willard, the Pottawatomie Ploughboy, at Havana Club, Cuba, on April 5, 1915. Over lunch in the Strand, Jack Curley, a boxing promoter representing a group of New York theatrical entrepreneurs who had put up the money, talked Johnson, and his then wife, Lucille, into returning home.

Johnson, in hindsight, appears like a piegeon being got ready for plucking by a group of sauve gentlemen anxious to cash in on the demand for a white world champion. For years they had sized up lumberjacks, dockers, miners, cowboys and the like to find a big enough specimen to stack against Johnson.

Willard, 6 ft. 6 in. – he became the tallest champion of all – came riding in from the wide open West, all 18 stone of him.

Johnson, then 37, was tired of being hounded out of his own country and, according to his own account was ready to 'do business'.

Johnson alleged that he was paid to throw the fight. Certainly the most published photo in heavyweight history – of Johnson appearing to shield his eyes from the blazing sun while taking the count in the 26th round – supports his story of fake.

But there were people around Johnson at the time who swear that athletic senility had simply caught up with him and that he dramatised the finish to offer an excuse.

Either way, Johnson was clobbered by a man who did not lace on a boxing glove until he was 28 years old and, who, at heart, was reckoned altogether too amiable for prize fighting.

Johnson raged that he was promised freedom from a trumped up conviction if he returned to the States and lost to Willard. He was assured – so he claimed – that the persecution would end. But if there is any truth in this story why did Johnson stay in the ring taking a fair amount of punishment until the 26th round?

Johnson had stipulated that the fight should be over 20 rounds and should take place in Mexico; that his payment should be 30,000 dollars in cash; that his wife be allowed to sit ringside; and that he should share the film rights. Not all of these things came to pass.

Scared by a story that bandits planned to hold him to ransom against the threat of delivering him to the U.S. Federal authorities, Johnson made a bee line for Cuba.

The fight, instead of 20 rounds had become 45 rounds – or fight to a finish. The film of it was banned in the USA and Johnson, hawking his copy of the celluloid round a war-torn Europe, found business well nigh impossible.

Richard J. Klegin, the backstage promoter behind Jack Curley, retired from the scene broke and fled from Cuba as a stowaway in a coal bunker.

The fight was staged before some 16,000 at a wooden race track named Oriental Park. It was, as it turned out, the last time a negro participated in a heavyweight championship bout until Joe Louis faced James J. Braddock 22 years later.

Willard was in fine condition, having trained for six months, while Johnson was showing spare tyre ridges around his middle. Johnson had just come from a theatrical tour of South America where his stints included pulling a team of horses and allowing a horse to stand on his chest.

Johnson later alleged there was no point in training hard for a fight he was to lose.

His answer to the question of why he stayed for 26 rounds before 'taking a dive' was that his wife was to receive a package of U.S. bills amounting to 50,000 dollars, in return for Johnson being counted out in the tenth round. She was to cue him when the money was handed over. His wife, says Jack, did not give the signal that the money had been handed over till just before the 26th round.

Lucille Johnson *did* leave the arena before the 26th round. Some observers suggested that she left merely because she knew that Johnson was beaten. Others suggested the money had been handed over, but it would not have been easy, with eyes frequently upon her, to have accepted a package of notes and concealed them without being noticed. There was also the risk, a strong one, too, of Lucille being mugged of the money before she even reached an exit.

Since Johnson had also asked for the money to be paid in 500 dollar bills, a denomination hardly likely to be handed over at the box offices, it helped discredit the story of a fixed fight.

In the fight business any match that does not end according to the general forecast tends to be labelled a put-up job. In fact, fixed fights are a rarity though anything goes in the American ring, and still does today. Mismatching is the easier way to assure the result of a fight.

Johnson's first words after the Havana hoo-ha were 'Willard was too much for me'. That may have been the simpler truth of the fight, but the slur of fix will always be there.

Jack Curley's recollections agree with what the deposed champion said – probably in a moment of truth. 'Nobody took Johnson's charges of fake seriously,' Curley said, 'Jack was past his prime. He was fat and dissipated, and he was worn down and knocked out by a strong, game, well-conditioned Willard.'

The victor added, 'If Johnson was going to throw it, he'd have throwed it sooner. It was as hot as hell in that ring.'

Throughout his life Johnson had suffered taunts that he 'couldn't take it'. His mother seems to have sown the first seeds of doubt when she said Jack was always losing school fights.

Sam Langford, who must have been an incredible man and, perhaps, the greatest non-champion of all, conceded nearly two stone to Johnson, (11 st. 4 lb. to 13 st. 3 lbs.), and was able to knock Johnson down, though not defeat him.

Stanley Ketchel, a middleweight champion of considerable punch power, also floored Johnson in a title fight at Colma, California, but Ketchel was clobbered within seconds of Johnson rising. The film of this fight shows that Johnson was loafing – a description frequently applied to him by scribe Fleischer – and was simply caught off guard.

Napping or not I could not imagine Joe Louis being put down by a middleweight like Rocky Graziano; or George Foreman or Muhammad Ali being toppled by, say Emile Griffith. Yet legend has it that a couple of Ketchel's teeth were buried in Johnson's right glove. Such flaws in Johnson's character as well as his fighting strengthen my belief that he was *not* the most fearsome heavyweight of all. He stood only 6 ft. and one-quarter-inch, and his best weight was 195 lb.

But Johnson was a master of defence. While his style gave the impression that he was toying with an opponent, he had an explosive leopard-like reflex which was often overwhelming.

There are numerous fights unlisted in Johnson's record, but early on in a career spanning 32 years he fought redoubtable Joe Choynski, (March 7, 1901), at Galveston and was close to defeating Choynski when the fight was stopped in the third round by Texas Rangers who arrested both contestants for creating a felony. They were jailed for 28 days.

For five years Johnson barnstormed America and became so proficient at his trade he was avoided as if he had leprosy. Shortage of opponents forced him to have several fights with the same men. His most notable opposition was Sam McVey and Sam Langford, negroes of exceptional skill, whom he met eight times between May 1905 and December 1906. He fought Joe Jeanette nine times, most of them 'no decision' bouts. There were times when Johnson was shoved into a ring with five other negroes and forced to fight to a finish. He was always the last man standing.

When he fought Sam McVey in San Francisco, in 1904, racialist rabble rousers flicked lighted cigarettes at Johnson's bare back but after knocking out McVey, Johnson deliberately kicked his bloodied corner bucket into the angry ringsiders and shouted, 'Allow me to serve the refreshments.' He vaulted the ropes and disappeared.

During Johnson's tempestuous career, nineteen people died in race riots that flared up because Johnson had smashed the best white fighters pitted against him.

Sandy Ferguson, a protegé of John L. Sullivan, was paired against Johnson, who had been threatened with his life unless he carried Ferguson. Instead, Johnson hammered Ferguson so badly that the humiliated loser savagely kicked Johnson in the groin – an action that, even in the States, constituted a foul.

The ring was torn down by a rioting crowd but Johnson beat his way safely to an exit. A week later Johnson fought Iron Man Joe Grim, so tough that his opponents were known to have fractured their hands in their vain attempts to knock him out. Johnson put Iron Joe down eighteen times.

Johnson's ring feats had struck fear into the heart of Canadian Tommy Burns, the smallest man to hold the world heavyweight championship, who sailed to fight in Australia. Johnson, spouting like a modern day Ali but with more venom, followed him.

The two bouts in Britain were no more than punch practice for Johnson and the National Sporting Club gentry – high class betting boys of their era – wanted to provide Johnson with his sea passage and expenses to Sydney provided he won the title and defended against Sam Langford in London.

Johnson's action in renaging from their agreement resulted in a colour-bar at the Club that virtually ruled the British boxing. (The Board of Control was not formed till 1929).

Johnson had been infuriated when called to the NSC Covent Garden headquarters and made to wait two hours. He was asked to strip for examination while cocktails were served and the 'Fancy' prodded his black body. It was not an official medical, merely a meaningless moment of humiliation for Johnson.

Having finally cornered Burns in Australia and the world title fight being guaranteed, Johnson used the lash of his tongue to such an extent that even the Aussies, normally connoisseurs of the outspoken remark, quickly decided that the intruder was intolerable.

But there may have been a publicist at work. Much printing ink was used round the world when Burns hurled an inkwell at Johnson during the preliminary rites of contract signing. Burns is alleged to have sneered, 'Hello, nigger,' while Johnson countered, 'So you've finally decided to stand and fight, you yellow Canuck ——.'

I don't set much store on these tales. The Promotion Industry was in its youth in those days but the basic principles of creating publicity, were already known and successfully practised, but Johnson and Burns really disliked each other, nobody disputed that.

The fight took place at Rushcutters Bay, Sydney, appropriately, on Boxing Day, 1908. Burns, surprisingly, was made a 3–2 favourite and many of his supporters were said to have arrived at the stadium carrying firearms and calling threats.

Burns was shorter than Rocky Marciano and though Johnson was not a giant of the modern proportions of Liston or Foreman, he dwarfed the stalking, crouch-style French Canadian whose real name was Noah Brusso.

From the opening round Johnson tormented Burns, cutting the champion's eyebrow and mouth. Burns took an eight count in the first round. Johnson waited with a hunter's patience to get his prey in his sights and brushed Burns's blows aside with contemptuous ease.

It was probably a disgustingly brutal fight to watch with nothing like the punch rate of modern bouts. Johnson waved a stars-and-stripes banner to taunt the crowd as well as Burns. If it was a patriotic gesture it was strangly quixotic, coming from a man detested by the bulk of his countryman and by a large proportion of his own race.

Johnson's hands were swift enough – so legend had it – to swat a fly in flight. He had no difficulty either in parrying or blocking Burns's desperate blows. By the seventh round Burns's nose was broken. The fight was grotesquely one-sided. Johnson dropped his hands (shades of Ali) and pointed to his stomach gesturing Burns 'Hit me here, Tahmmy'.

Author Jack London, reporting the fight for an American syndicated column, wrote ... 'It was hopeless, preposterous, heroic! Johnson play-acted all the time. Burns was a mere toy in his hands, a pygmy against a colossus. ...'

The publicity pedlars had said this would be the Fight of the Century!

The promoter was Hugh McIntosh, nicknamed Huge Deal. Prudently he was also serving as referee. McIntosh allowed the taunting chat to continue through 14 laborious rounds with Johnson rebuking Burns, in the twelfth, 'You ain't showed me nothing yet.'

A ringsider yelled, 'Even money Burns is there at the finish,' and Johnson yelled back, 'A hundred to one he don't black my eye!'

When Burns had been reduced to a pitiful punchbag and had taken another count in the fourteenth, the police entered the ring to save the champion from further injury. McIntosh was pleased to use this as the excuse to raise Johnson's hand as the first official black heavyweight champion.

Jack London, guilty of pouring forth the hyperbole that we boxing writers continue to inflict on our readers ('a dew-drop had more chance than he with the giant Ethiopian') called for the comeback of sizeable Jim Jeffries. Jeffries, a white man, was called on to emerge from his alfalfa farm and remove the golden smile from Johnson's face. 'Jeff, it's up to you,' he wrote. The description White Hope was born.

Being world champion inflamed white hatred for Johnson. He was described as 'the black shadow on American boxing' – a description which in today's more tolerant climate was unashamed racial prejudice. One wonders how America would have rated Johnson had he been white. It would probably have hailed and hoorayed him as a hero, the most skilful and fearsome fighter of all time.

Britain had had enough of Johnson and *The Times,* perhaps foreshadowing the events of Notting Hill in the sixties, referred to him as 'a flash nigger' while the London County Council flatly refused a promoter a licence to stage a fight between Johnson and popular Bombardier Billy Wells. The LCC, no doubt, did dear old Billy, who had a touch of china in his chin, a great favour.

Johnson returned to a vaudeville tour with a medley of bag punching, sparring and slapping a bass, an instrument he played by ear.

He returned to the ring less than three months after beating Burns to dispose of Victor McLaglen (the only Oscar winner to have fought for the world heavyweight title). This was followed by three no-decision bouts and the mismatch against middleweight Ketchel.

Meanwhile, the one-time boilermaker Jeffries was being lured back to action. At 35, and short of competition, Jeffries was soft bellied and could not give Johnson much of a fight. But he lasted fifteen rounds and was beaten by a technical k.o. at Reno on July 4, 1910.

The fight was so exhaustingly reported and discussed, including an unlikely after-fight allegation that Jeffries had been given poisoned tea, that thousands of ghetto negroes throughout the States danced in the streets when the result was known. Six were killed and scores injured in serious rioting. If only Johnson had had the simple foresight to have been born with a white skin! He left Reno clutching a satchel containing 60,000 dollars. Johnson had sacked his manager, Sam Fitzpatrick, this had been widely regarded as evidence of ingratitude and conceit.

Again Jack London, who seemed both fascinated and infuriated by Johnson, as some authors today are transfixed by Muhammad Ali, was using a prosaic pen. 'No one understands him, this man who smiles. Well, the story of the fight is the story of a smile. If ever a man won by nothing more fatiguing than a smile, Johnson won today.'

The smile was brightened by the champion having a

diamond inserted in his teeth to match the sparkle that came from his walking-cane top. He wore velvet suits, learned to speak French, German and Spanish and reckoned Shakespeare was a bum writer for plotting to have Othello bumped off. He learned to quote Spencer and Chaucer.

But one thing Johnson never did learn to do was to keep his mouth shut.

After boxing, wrestling, bullfighting and enjoying the company of a hard drinking rebel General in Mexico, Johnson pined for the U.S. – and Chicago in particular. He was bored with continually being on the run.

But the charge of transporting a white woman across state lines, had not been dropped. With his usual incorrigible – and irrational – optimism he made himself believe that some benevolent genie would appear to settle his argument with the law. When Johnson surrendered to the Federal authorities in San Diego on July 20, newspaper headline type went up to Armistice Day size. Johnson hoped for leniency and showed willing to change his ways. But the sentence stood. He was sent to serve one year and a day at The Walls, the penitentiary at Leavenworth, Kansas. He became a prison celebrity and five heavyweights were brought for brief visits while Johnson fought them to entertain the inmates.

His cell became a hotel room and Johnson hired his own cook. He kept a good supply of booze and cigars and when the day came for his release (he had remission for good behaviour), he addressed the prisoners and was escorted to the gates by a brass band and the ex-Governor of Nevada, Denver. S. Dickerson who had befriended Johnson.

Johnson could act in a boxing ring with the nonchalance most of us would feel in a barber's chair and he lasted far longer than any other heavyweight. His art and the marvellous instant reflex defence, never deserted him. At 48 he could still defeat a previously unbeaten young heavyweight, Pat Lester, in Mexico over fifteen rounds.

He was 50 when he appeared in his last official fight,

losing a decision to Bill Hartwell, in Kansas City, in 1928. He had the audacity to box exhibition bouts until 1945.

Johnson's extraordinary reflex had also saved him from death on numerous occasions when he drove at dangerous speeds in big cars. Being behind a wheel and totally in charge always heightened Johnson's arrogance. Approaching the age of 70 Johnson was slowing down, mentally and physically, but never admitted it. He still drove at high speeds as though as a gesture of rebuke to society. He would be second to no man.

On June 10, 1946, at the wheel of a 1939 Lincoln Zephyr, heading from North California to New York after a small engagement with a travelling circus in Texas, Johnson swerved at speed to avoid an approaching lorry and crashed into a pylon.

His passenger, Fred Scott, employed to keep him company, was thrown clear. The old champ was unconscious in a crumpled car and taken to St Agnes Hospital, Raleigh, where he died from internal injuries.

The young medicos who attended Johnson had no idea who he was. He was just another sad road casualty registered in the death book as 'Male, black, elderly, carrying licence name J. Arthur.'

When it was discovered that the legendary Johnson had been killed, his body was shipped to Chicago where 2,500 mourners – many of them white – waited to parade past his open coffin at a mortuary in South Michigan Ave.

In death Jack Johnson had become a hero.

6

Rocky Marciano

The rags-to-riches gravy train of Rocky Marciano ran on traditional rails : beginning as a strong, undisciplined punch swinger to retirement as the only unbeaten heavyweight champion of the world. All along the line there was a dual personality : the gentle man outside the ring, with a high pitched, almost apologetic voice ; and inside the ring, a fighter aptly described by veteran columnist, Peter Wilson, as the Twentieth Century Caveman.

Marciano's tragic death on August Bank Holiday, 1969, on the eve of his 46th birthday, was mourned around the world. He was killed, with two friends, in a private plane crash at Newton, Iowa, on his way from Florida. He left a wife, a 16-year-old daughter, a 17-month-old son and millions of admirers. Even in London, where Marciano never fought, a memorial service was arranged by members of the British boxing fraternity and the Boxing Writer's Club. Don Cockell, the blacksmith whom Marciano had nearly compressed in a lop-sided world title fight, was a church usher for the service. Henry Cooper read the lesson. Marciano commanded that kind of respect.

Only a few months earlier Rocky, complete with toupée, had won his last fight – seen by more millions than in his heyday. It was the world wide televised computer 'fight' against Muhammad Ali, (Cassius Clay), a gimmick that I found unpalatable, but millions enjoyed it. It was a well-staged, privately filmed encounter with a carefully guarded

ending, allegedly decided by facts fed into a computer. The
machine decided Rocky, cut up as expected, would come off
the floor to win by a knock-out. Ali, to his credit, made the
'end' look realistic.

Marciano, a slave to training in his prime, had done his
utmost to whip his sturdy frame into reasonably physical
condition – a hearty eater struggling to win his battle
of the bulge. He treated the cod fight seriously. Marciano did not want to be remembered as a loser and in
the event, the masses saw lovable Rocky go out in customary
glory.

The previous live-TV occasion had been in 1953 – a fight
that lasted less than one round against Jersey Joe Walcott.
All Marciano's other battles were confined to delayed show-
ings.

As an unbeatable champion, Marciano's career seemed to
disprove the axiom that skill must be a component of success.
His impact was the impact of brute strength, of almost
animal crudity. His punch mocked the very concept of craft
or skill. But unanswerable as his punch, and the success,
may have seemed I have always doubted that he could have
laid a winning glove on a Muhammad Ali at his peak. Many
pundits would place the popular Marciano above the controversial Clay-turned-Ali. You can't beat an unbeaten
record.

Rocky was a superbly managed, shrewdly trained heavyweight who often heaved punches like cobblestones and fought
as though he looked on the referee as a personal insult. He
reigned supreme from 1952 until 1956 and within three
years was elected to boxing's Hall of Fame. He scored 43
knock-outs or stoppages in 49 fights.

The two men chiefly responsible for Marciano's success
have also passed on. Al Weill was his manager, Al of the
Punch-like appearance and soup stained waistcoat; a man
of acumen who made matches for the then powerful International Boxing Club in New York. Al suffered a mental

breakdown after losing Rocky's friendship, and died in Miami.

Dapper Charley Goldman, who was English-born, (he wore a black bowler), had been a top bantam weight in his day. He taught Rocky all he knew. Charley showed Rocky how to overcome the disadvantage of short arms, he had a mere 68 in. reach, (the shortest in heavyweight history), and pound an opponent's body until the head fell off. Charley and Rocky liked each other.

It was Rocky's wife, Barbara, his father, Pierino, and a punch landed by ancient Archie Moore that convinced the ring's iron man he should quit at the top.

'I was training in camp to fight Moore in 1955 and my wife visited me with our young daughter. She was screaming, "Don't you hit my Daddy" when I was sparring and when I went to cuddle her she kinda shied away from me. It was a sad experience and one I didn't like,' said Marciano.

'I began to realise it was taking me more time than usual to really get into top fighting shape. I needed perfect physical condition. I didn't compare with the Ray Robinson's of this world but I could hit a bit and as long as I could keep going forward I could catch up with the trickier guys.

'I'd had 46 stitches in my face after fighting Ezzard Charles in 1954. My nose had been sliced clean through. I still don't know how Charley stopped the bleeding. To fight to a 15-round finish in that condition takes something out of a man. I was virtually out for three or four days afterwards. I'd thought about retiring then. But I was tempted to fight Archie Moore, such a good guy and great fighter. Thirty-five seconds after leaving the corner I found myself on the floor looking up at a man ten years older than me. He'd beaten me to the punch. It was the hardest punch I'd taken.

'Rocky, I thought, this is going to be one hell of a good fight. I caught up with Archie in the ninth and remember saying 'Sorry' when I finally nailed him. But I knew that would be the end. I wasn't leading a normal life. The nagging of training, the discipline, the way Weill treated me, the parting from my family, it was all too much.

'I wasn't scared of anyone and when I gave it up it got to be hard to refuse a million dollars to make a comeback to fight Floyd Patterson.

'But my Pa would come to the training camp and plead with me to pack up. It was he who influenced me most. He used to enjoy himself coming to the training camps. But not near the end. He'd changed. He'd say, "You want me to live a little longer, Rocky? I watch you train, I watch you sacrifice and I can't stand it any more." I'm glad I got out when I did. My pal, Jimmy Cerniglia, a wealthy man, used to kid me he'd run me over if I made a comeback.'

Marciano sacrificed many of the good things in life to become the biggest force in boxing. 'Without boxing where would I have been?' I recall him saying, 'I'd probably have worked in a shoe factory like my Pa. I could never figure me marrying a rich woman. I did it right while I had the chance and then got out.'

He will always be admired for his retirement decision. He was genuinely admired as a person.

Born Rocco Francis Marchegiano, sixth child of Pierino and Pasqualina, on September 1, 1924, he was brought up in Peyton Place county, Brockton, Massachusetts. His parents had emigrated from Italy shortly before World War One.

Rocky was built more like a wrestler than a fighter and with hardly any boxing going on in the staid New England area it seemed he would never climb into a ring. His parents disapproved of the sport. The dutiful son had a varied and not too profitable career as a semi-professional footballer, baseball catcher, dishwasher, shoemaker, road gang navvy, truck driver's mate, gas-pipe layer and general help-mate to a family of two brothers and three sisters.

When finally launched into prize fighting he was ditch-digging at Brockton. They soon tagged him the Brockton Blockbuster.

Perhaps Rocky's prowess was first established of all places, at a Swansea (South Wales) pub. He was embarrassed to repeat the tale. But the first apprentice effort at pugilism paid off.

It appears an Australian soldier was spouting about the deficiencies of American soldiers within earshot of the rookie G.I. Marciano who was combating the rigours of warm beer.

The story acquired all sorts of embellishments when Marciano later became champion of the world, but it was nothing more than a barrack-style punch-up. Against his will Rocky, ('I was just a fat little Italian,') was elected by his comrades to take up arms in defence of the Yanks. Rocky chose the left arm and hooked the unsuspecting Aussie into oblivion. He was delighted at the time, a little sorry afterwards. 'I wasn't really the trouble shooting type,' he said. He left Wales to escort G.I. supplies for the Normandy second front but was encouraged to persevere with Army boxing.

The Marciano we saw was a tutored Marciano. The untutored one must have been something else. He is known to have missed with a punch so wild that he fell on his knees. His expression at such moments was a mixture of embarrassment and injured innocence as though his opponent wasn't quite playing the game.

'Hey, you ducked,' Rocky seemed to be accusing.

He lost in the 1945 AAU championships at Portland, against Joe De Angelis and broke a knuckle bone. He was disqualified against Ted Lester for accidently kicking him, having fallen against a slack rope which threw his leg up! He is also recorded as losing a decision to Coley Wallace, a good looking negro who later turned pro and depicted the part of Joe Louis in a film about the great Brown Bomber. That was the final of the Golden Gloves tournament in 1948.

These were the only blots in an otherwise unstoppable career. Sports-minded Americans, always yearning for a white hope, exploded into dollar spinning ecstacies when Rocky came out fighting.

The New Englanders began to believe that the windmill style ex-G.I. was the answer to the promoters' prayer and Rocky's neighbour, Allie Colombo, wrote to the 'Garden' matchmaker, Al Weill, suggesting a trial bout. Rocky and Allie hitch-hiked to Manhattan. The manager forgot to send the fare.

Mr Weill, more impressed by Marciano's stomach muscles than stoicism, showed him where to sign the dotted line and agreed to let him have 50 per cent of all Al could earn. The initial work-out was a disaster, but Weill never turned down a man with muscles and a fighting heart. Especially one of Italian stock.

Marciano astonished the ringside cognoscenti by wrapping his head in his arms allowing his sparring partner to hammer his ribs without let or hindrance. Marciano's astonishing explanation was: 'That's the way I fight. If a guy hits you in the belly you let him keep doing it until he gets tired.'

The pint-sized Goldman was assigned to put some semblance of defence into Marciano's fighting and if possible even more dynamite into his punches. One Harry Balzerian was assigned as the first victim of the newly designed Marciano at a place called, appropriately, Providence, Rhode Island, in July 1948. Balzerian wilted within two minutes. He was the start to a long line of wilters. His first recorded fight, under the management of Gene Caggiano, was a three-round win over Lee Epperson at Holyoke.

It may be argued that the astute Mr Weill, who would often publicly scathe and humiliate the easy going Marciano, was excessively cautious in his choice of heavyweights for Marciano to ply his trade upon.

It was, in fact, the sensible way to build-up the potential world beater. Confidence Marciano always had. Craft could only come with experience. As heavyweights go, Rocky was not big. He was inside 6ft. and his best weight was 184 lb. (13 st. 2 lb.). He was tiny compared to Ali or George Foreman, and he was a lot lighter than Joe Frazier. But the weight was compressed into brawny arms and biceps, where hitting power starts. Marciano's forearm hitting was estimated to be greater than some heavyweights can deliver with their full body force going into a punch. I have never accepted however, the theory that Rocky deliberately landed blows on an opponent's arms to cause instant tiredness. It was simply the way Marciano fought. He would, no doubt, have preferred to select specific, (and more vulnerable), targets for his blows, but such refinements had never been programmed in Rocky's genes. The only approach he had was punch saturation, a sort of preposterous, irresistible, overwhelming frontal assault.

The highlight of Rocky's career must have been catching up with Jersey Joe Walcott, whose size and skill alike were awesome.

Walcott had learned his trade in the lean years. His record is unavailable before 1930 when he k.o.'d a character called Cowboy Wallace at Camden. Walcott had beaten the giant Joe Baksi (who wrecked Bruce Woodcock and Freddie Mills in London) and twice outpointed world light-heavyweight champion, Joey Maxim. When Walcott was adjudged a 15-rounds points loser against the national hero, Joe Louis, in 1947, the verdict was booed. But, at 37, Jersey Joe became world heavyweight champion by defeating the vastly under-rated Ezzard Charles. Walcott repeated the victory and, fourteen months after winning the title, defended it against the new hero Marciano at Philadelphia.

No man approaching his 40th year should have been allowed in the same city as a fit Marciano, let alone in the same ring, but Jersey Joe came close indeed to achieving the impossible. For the best part of 13 rounds the old boy feinted, jabbed and outsmarted the rough-hewn Rock. Twenty-three years of pro campaigning were packed into that title defence. Marciano was being made to look a mug, and Walcott was ahead on the cards of the three officials.

But a big puncher is never beaten until the final bell and Rocky was able to throw the best blow of his career to flatten Walcott; the perfect k.o.

Walcott, a God-fearing, father-of-six had been able to see most of Marciano's punches coming. Manager Weill was becoming testier than ever, watching his big hope being shown up. The hunk of granite was being chipped to pieces. But if there was one quality Rocky had as well as crude force it was perseverance and in the end it paid off. Walcott was waging the finest battle of his career. In the opening round he left-hooked the raw Marciano for the first count of his 43-fight career, but Rocky clambered up at 'four' and resumed pitching punches. Only a year earlier Ezzard Charles had succumbed to that same Walcott left hook.

Coming up for the 13th round, Marciano's face, as they say, was looking worse for wear. His scalp was gashed, his left eye bled, his lips were swollen. The oldest heavyweight champion of them all looked a good bet to keep the title.

Trainer Goldman had repeatedly pleaded to Marciano to slip inside the Walcott guard and plant the sledgehammer right that Charley had nicknamed Suzie Q. But the veteran was too cagey to be caught. Then came the mistake and Marciano's counter. Walcott had backed into the ropes and was waiting to counter with cobra-quickness when Marciano lunged at him.

Walcott cocked his left hook, exposed his chin, and, propped against the ropes, was unable to pull his body backwards. It was Joe's big blunder, Marciano unleashed his right at that moment and it reached the target first. The blow landed flush on Walcott's jaw. His face contorted and his body crumbled. A lifeless left arm hung entangled over the bottom rope and his head was twisted back 'looking down his own spine – sightlessly', Peter Wilson reported from the ringside. Walcott was out to the world. That one punch had wiped out the arrears. Marciano, at 28, became the new heavyweight champion with, perhaps, the most ferocious single punch in the history of the division.

Crude, awkward, styleless, but utterly dependable and immovable, that was Marciano. The first man to win the heavyweight title without first suffering defeat. Hunger for success and the family struggle had inspired him. He had arrived just too early to reap the benefit of the nation-wide closed-circuit TV, but his seven title fights grossed 1,500,000 dollars (then £535,700) for the Rock.

The inevitable return fight was arranged seven months later and this time the ageing Walcott probably suffered stage fright. He went out in the first round after just 2 minutes 25 seconds. It was Jersey Joe's last fight.

Manager Weill, always on the lookout for opponents likely to draw a crowd but not too much blood, picked on Britain's Don Cockell when the Rock had begun to punch himself out of work. The two wars against Ezzard Charles had earned Marciano his glory and it was time to taper off.

Training rigours, probably harder than any other champion endured, had begun to take the mental edge off the Rock. Physically he remained reinforced concrete, but mentally there was doubt, hesitation, insecurity. The fact that defeat would be the price of the slightest slacking off. His style demanded total aggression and this could be sustained only at the very peak of physical perfection. The style and strategy which other fighters could call on were not available to Rocky. The craft and subtlety that a Moore, a Walcott, or an Ali could switch on when occasion demanded were attributes that lay over the edge of Rocky's map of the world. Indeed his head-down technique would probably have caused instant disqualification under British or European rules. Teddy Waltham, long-time top British referee and ex-secretary of the British Boxing Board of Control, openly told Marciano that his method of fighting, though not deliberately flouting the rules, would not be tolerated in Britain.

Weill, of course, never had the slightest intention of turning his man-eating tiger loose outside the States. There Rocky was assured of the closest protection from referees, though of course it was Marciano's victims who needed the protection. American refereeing, particularly in California, is generally sound but there are occasions when rule books seem to have been printed with invisible ink.

Such an occasion was the Kezar Stadium, San Francisco, when Marciano, to use a Cockney expression, took a diabolical liberty with courageous Don Cockell.

Cockell had gone into the fight as the usual no-hoper Limey, laughed at and labelled Fat Boy. The British champion, who started as a blacksmith and still pounds an anvil in Surrey, had a finely shaped physique during his reign as light-heavyweight champion. But the after-effects of glandular fever played havoc with his frame and no matter how hard Cockell trained he could never shake off the roly-poly figure.

But there was nothing wrong with Cockell's ticker. He'd told manager John Simpson that, under no circumstances must he stop the fight. He'd fight until he dropped, and he did.

Cockell was the only Marciano opponent shorter than the champion. The Don, as we called him, had surprising agility and he was able to outbox the champion right up to the time when Marciano's clubbing fists took the steam out of Don's legs. It was not only the fists that caused the damage. Marciano bore in like a billygoat and the crown of Cockell's head was cut. 'A deliberate butt,' hollered Cockell's cornermen. 'The referee never warned Marciano. The cut was caused by a left uppercut,' countered Weill. That I would like to have seen!

Cockell, to his credit, never complained about Rocky's tactics. He still doesn't. 'That's the way the man fought.

He couldn't 'arf punch,' Cockell says, 'He didn't complain if you did the same to him.'

Even the most rabid Marciano fan at that San Francisco ringside could hardly have described his hero's activity as boxing. When Cockell slumped to the canvas on one knee a punch so late it practically started a round earlier crashed into the Briton's face. Nobody wanted to see a world title change hands by disqualification, but a word in Marciano's ear would not have been amiss. Referee Frankie Brown, however, judged that the punch was on its way as the bell rang and bad luck for Cockell.

Cockell heaved his 14 st. 9 lb. body off the floor and came back for more. But the man-eating Marciano, a primeval battering animal, kept thumping away ignoring acknowledged target areas and, sometimes, having trouble hearing the bell to finish the round. It was certainly dangerous for Don to drop his hands at the bell. Rocky was notorious as an after-timer.

After 54 seconds of the ninth round Cockell was halted having stood four square to the storm. He was defenceless yet prepared to fight on. Marciano admired him for it. Ex-fighter, Willie Ritchie, of the Californian Commission, said: 'Cockell is one of the greatest guys who ever trod this earth.'

'Don didn't really look like a fighter, but he was deceptive,' said Marciano, 'He was dead game. I'd call him a powder puff puncher but my best punches didn't seem to affect him. He could hit pretty quick. Certainly he was one of the gamest guys I fought.'

The final curtain of Marciano's career came as it began – with a knock-out win. Archie Moore, the light-heavyweight king, had conducted a personal publicity campaign with 'Wanted' adds. and a number printed on Marciano's chest. Newspapers lapped it up. Moore offered a 10,000 dollar reward to anyone who could get him a fight with Marciano. The old Mongoose was setting the trap. Rocky, of course, would have taken on Archie at the drop of a hat but they snarled at each other long enough to make certain of a big gate. The fight was a natural. It took place in New York on September 21, 1955.

During the build-up for the fight with Cockell word had it that a sparring partner, Toxie Hall, had been fired from the Marciano camp for knocking the boss down. There was the usual scepticism of a publicity stunt because ticket sales were slow, but often in boxing the truth is 'twisted by knaves to make a trap for fools'.

The sparring partner did drop Marciano – and he later admitted it. A lax moment in sparring and Rocky was toppled. Archie Moore was getting old but he could hit with rifle accuracy.

When Marciano was felled in round two he pitched face forward and Moore claimed that referee Harry Kessler prevented him from taking instant advantage of the knockdown. The wiping of resin from the gloves, the peering into Marciano's eyes, accounted for vital seconds while Archie was peering over Kessler's shoulder anxiously awaiting the signal to carry on firing.

The years of spartan existence and the fierce pride of Marciano's overcame the superior skills of Moore. 'I never hit Archie a good punch until the seventh round,' I recall Rocky saying. But when the end came in the ninth, Moore was in no condition to argue. Like the majority of Marciano's fights the finish was merciless and complete.

Moore had been down for four counts after having smashed Marciano with all he had. A doctor wanted to pull Archie out of the fight after the sixth, but he made a brave stand. He was saved by the bell in the eighth and finally went down in the ninth under the last fearsome barrage Marciano was ever to deliver in the ring.

The knockdown that Moore scored – a blow harder than any delivered in 19 hungry pro years – and the terrible nose injury Marciano suffered against Charles were factors in the retirement announced on April 27, 1956. No man is im-

pervious to punishment and Rocky Marciano was big enough
to acknowledge it.

Rocky, as I have emphasised and perhaps over-emphasised,
had glaring ring deficiencies but when such expert ringmen
as Walcott, Charles and Moore could not contain him, a
place among the Great ones was assured.

I recall another Marciano victory that made hard men
weep. He knocked out mighty Joe Louis in the eighth round
of a non-title match designed to promote Rocky's strength
and convince the plump 15 st. 2¾ lb. Louis that he should
not continue boxing merely because the tax collector was
becoming a nuisance. It was Louis' last fight, October 26,
1951, and the balding Brown Bomber had to be assisted
out of the ring. Charley Goldman had gambled that Joe's
experience might overcome the 37-fight Marciano. The
trainer was wrong. They made Louis a 7–5 favourite, the
shortest ever laid on Joe. For six rounds the remarkable
'Bomber' managed to stave off the Rock and pinch the points.
But in the eighth, Rocky got inside, where his strength took
command, and battered Louis insensible. The final right sent
poor Joe sprawling through the ropes, his head striking the
ring apron, while a compassionate photographer tried to
cradle the head of a past champion that everyone admired.
Rocky gave the impression of wanting to pick Louis up. His
brutal job had been done, he felt compassion and little sense
of glory. Referee Rugby Goldstein refused to count and
signalled the fight was over. He spared Joe the indignity of
an official count out.

'Marciano hurt every time he landed a punch. He's so
powerful my arms ached blocking punches.' said Louis. This
fight helped to 'make' Marciano but typical of his humility
Rocky never claimed credit. 'I beat only the shadow of the
real Joe Louis,' he'd say.

There was a remarkable sensitivity about the hardest
heavyweight of them all. He'd apologise if an opponent considered Rocky had struck a foul blow. He required a doctor's

attention because he was so emotionally overcome when hearing of the assassination of President Kennedy, whom Marciano knew and admired.

It was a fitting tribute to Marciano that modern gladiators turned out en masse around the world to mourn the passing of the most successful of their kind.

7

Archie Moore

You could count on the thumbs of two boxing gloves the number of modern-era boxers who qualify for election to the gallery of immortals. Archie Moore is one. Sportswriters were milling around a steamy gymnasium in Kingston, Jamaica, in January 1973, wrestling with the problem of picking the winner between Joe Frazier, unbeaten and seemingly indestructible, and a then untested and unbeaten George Foreman, for the world heavyweight championship.

'Foreman will knock him out and quick. Its a no-contest,' said greying haired Archie Moore who was among Foreman's hired helpers. There was a moment's silence and a pretentious listener questioned Archie 'But why should you say that?' Moore fixed a firm eye as though he were measuring the shortest distance for a punch to the jaw, and snapped, 'Because I'm an expert, Sir, that's why,' and he was, and still is.

Moore's record does not give a complete analysis of the man who knew more angles than Euclid, but he is listed as scoring the record number of knockouts in major competition by the *Ring Encyclopedia* – 141 failing to finish in 229 recorded contests. He beat the existing record of Young Stribling who had 126 knockouts.

'My aunt once told me, "If the labour is big or small, do it well or not at all," ' Moore has said. He sure did. His career record begins in 1936, days when many fights went unrecorded, when he made 35-dollar appearances in desert towns. As a result, he allegedly claimed the Kansas,

Oklahoma, and Missouri middleweight titles in 1937. His age was also a matter of contention.

Archibald Lee Wright was born in Benoit, Miss., on December 13, 1913, according to his mother who was there at the time. But Archie, who took the name Moore from foster parents, argues it was in 1916 and at Collinsville, Illinois. 'I decided I was three when I was born,' he says. But what we do know for certain is that Moore was given the ring runaround for years because he was too good for his own good and did not get a world title chance until 1952. He won, of course, at his first attempt, against Joey Maxim.

In 1963 'The Mongoose' was still fighting and was 50 when he bowed out, well, maybe only 48, and against an obscure foe named Mike DiBiase at Phoenix, Arizona. Archie wanted to walk out with a knockout win and he did – after being floored in four in his previous fight, as predicted, by a then Cassius Clay. Masterly Moore had taught Clay tricks at his San Diego (Calif.) training centre he called The Salt Mine.

Even the boastful Clay-turned-Ali would not dare to claim that he beat Archie Moore. He knocked out the shadow of a great boxer who was in effect aspiring to no more than just making a fast buck in his twilight years. He had, after all, been the most elderly champion in history.

But it took ancient Arch a long time to conclude that he was better off retiring in the distinguished company of his contemporaries Joe Louis, Jersey Joe Walcott, Rocky Marciano, etc. Some of these had accumulated paunches and tried to disguise the fact. Archie, in contrast, made fun of his greying hair.

'The old guy should quit, look at his grey head!' Moore heard an apprentice say as he worked out in a Los Angeles gym. 'It isn't the grey head that worries you young fellows,' Moore countered, 'it's these old grey fists.'

Because Moore's build was undistinguished and his countenance unscarred there was nothing about his appearance that hinted at the rough, sometimes violent nature of his trade for 27 years, or more. He was more typecast, I thought, when he played the poor, gentle character of Jim The Slave in Huckleberry Finn. Archie was convincing on the screen, he'd been a strolling player all his life.

He often sported a wispy bebop goatee that gave him more the look of a jazz musician than a prize fighter. His ring apparel was gaudy, and even when he appears in a boxer's corner he still wears something way-out like denims and bright headgear that looks more like a tea-cosy than a hat.

I have seen Archie in ankle length, gold lamee dressing gowns; in a gown festooned with sequins; and in grey topper and tails like some potentate at the Epsom Derby. In Jamaica he wore a white dinner jacket and carried a cane.

Moore called himself The Mongoose and although he was (and still is) agile, sharp sighted and fearless, like a mongoose, he had none of the irritable habits of that ferocious little fighter. Children respond to Moore enthusiastically. Wherever he goes, from Toronto to Tasmania, Archie is greeted and complimented on his happy disposition.

He has chatted with President Eisenhower and been photographed with Juan Peron – the dictator's arms around him. He is known to have been disappointed at not receiving a summons to Buckingham Palace when he defended the world light-heavyweight championship in London against Yolande Pompey. He trained at Windsor. 'I really dig that historic stuff, you know. I am not a politician but an ambassador of goodwill,' he told me.

In reality Moore isn't quite the political innocent he pretends to be. He has helped in the Democratic cause these last 30 years as a citizen of good standing in San Diego. Over-training was not always Moore's way in his professional life, but he had always done what was necessary. For his first fight at the polls however, he couldn't train at all. He was out of the country defending his title when canvassing for votes was of greater importance. When Moore took out his nomination papers he listed his birthplace as Mississippi on one and Missouri on another. When advised that he would have to make a choice he protested on the grounds that both states deserved the honour!

For years Moore had running feuds with various boxing commissions, chiefly the World Boxing Association who failed to give him sufficient grace as champion, and he appealed to the United Nations.

'When I wanted the NBA (later WBA) to recognise me as the rightful world title challenger, they let me wither for five solid years,' he argued.

The self-appointed, politically motivated body twice defrocked Moore when the world knew he was the real champion. They even nominated Harold Johnson for the title and Moore had beaten him four out of five meetings.

Moore had a succession of managers; from a character called Kid Bandy to the famous Jimmy (Boy Bandit) Johnston; his brother, Charlie; and Jack (Doc) Kearns. But it was usually astute Archie who did his own campaigning to get championship fights. Putting opponents out was never too much trouble, but getting them in the ring – that was hard going. He spent 50,000 dollars distributing a 'Wanted' style poster which offered a reward to the man who could guarantee him a fight with Rocky Marciano. Most people would have paid a ransom for Rocky not to fight them. Archie got his wish and still has the poster framed at his home.

He failed in heavyweight title bouts against Marciano and Floyd Patterson – though he defeated some heavies like Nino Valdes, a Cuban who wrecked Joe Erskine in Britain, and whom many thought was worthy of a world championship.

Talking was Moore's game long before the garrulous Ali-Clay claimed the attention of the media, but though Archie's words could often hit home he had a disarming manner in delivering them. When he knocked out a fancied young opponent, Tony Anthony, in 1957, the loser's manager commented, 'Archie is a smart old guy, he talked his way to victory'. To which Moore replied, 'I should remind the gentleman that I also mixed a few punches with the conversation'.

Words, Archie insisted, were his only excess during those hectic ring years. His boxing was always an exercise in calculated economy. Few punches were wasted. Each one had to pay its way. He mounted an unorthodox, crisscross defence, tucking his face behind his biceps, often allowing an enthusiastic opponent partly to punch himself out while Archie considered the counter-moves. His punch deliveries were perfect – short, sharp and anything but sweet – and most of the men of his size, 141 of them to be precise, got the message.

Occasionally Archie's tremendous fondness for food would blow his frame to rotund proportions. At such times it was difficult to believe that he could shock his body, as he did over and over again, into shedding up to two stones (28 lb.) and then go into a ring and defeat a younger man in prime athletic condition.

He defied all the ring rituals of dieting and had us believe that he had learned his trick of instant slimming from an Australian aborigine. This was in his Down Under period when he campaigned in Australia after being driven out of America in the Forties due to a lack of fights. Because Moore was a natural joker few believed him, but there appears to be some truth in his claim. (He is, after all, an expert.) Aboriginals it seems will carry meat while roaming the bush, chew the blood out, and then restore the meat without swallowing. I have seen Moore chewing without swallowing. When he was making drastic efforts to come in at 12 st. 7 lb. to fight Pompey at Harringay Arena in 1956, he dined daily at Isow's Restaurant in Soho and would carefully place his chewed steak in a napkin and whispered to the waiter that the meat was too tough. He had the management nearly in tears while he kept his act going. He also kept a small pharmacy of laxatives in his bathroom. One way or another he never failed to make the required weight to defend his title.

But there were times when Archie almost missed being the Wizard of the One Oz – the ounce he liked to scale inside the championship limit. Sniffing for a pre-fight story for my paper on the morning of Moore's battle with Pompey, I waited outside a Turkish bath in Jermyn St, off Piccadilly, for Moore to finish sweating only a half hour before he reported for the weigh-in. This was in a sleazy, basement dance club (the disco was still unborn) opposite the famous Windmill Theatre where they never clothed. Archie apparently admired my door-stepping (the blight of a reporter's life) but tried to persuade me to write that he had merely been getting his pants pressed! My accusation that gluttony could have caused this weight problem brought a reply, with all possible solemnity; 'I am not a glutton, I am an explorer of food!' Trouble was that Archie was particularly attracted to starch and fries – nutritional lands best left unexplored by champions with a weighty problem. Fat, reckoned Archie, was just a three letter word invented to confuse people.

With Moore in his fortieth year, the strain of reducing had started to show. He had to conserve his remaining strength to pace for a scheduled 15-rounds. He was dicing with his title and he knew it. Pompey, from Trinidad, whom I had written about when he was a mere preliminary performer in London, was superbly built though it is possible that his muscle structure by its very magnificence slowed his reflexes, boxers need suppleness.

The fight took place on June 5, 1956, and when Moore was merely taking stock at the start London referee, Jack Hart, who was also a licensed bookmaker, stopped the 'fight' and insisted upon more action. 'I thought the ref was very rude,' said Moore afterwards.

For eight rounds Moore stalked, parried punches, offered his tantalising defence, and was trailing. His cornermen became angry. I sat within hearing distance of Moore's corner. 'Let's go to work, you'll blow the title,' manager Johnston kept saying. 'Don't worry,' Moore answered, 'It'll be O.K.'

But Moore was not carrying Pompey. He was afraid to put on a pressure spell in case Pompey came back. Moore knew he had only the strength to land his famous finishing punches; he did not have enough to sustain a softening-up process as well. He knew that Pompey could take a good punch. Moore had measured Pompey's reaction in the fourth when he unleashed a succession of blows to establish his superiority. It was a rehearsal for the finale.

By round eight Moore was ready for action. Pompey had won the seventh to put him ahead, but a cut over his left eye was the beginning of the end. I heard Moore say, 'I got something to work on,' before the eighth, but afterwards he addressed the interviewers with, 'It was very unfortunate that my opponent should be injured.'

Pompey's right eye was swollen in the ninth and the end was near. Though Pompey shook the champion at the start of the tenth, Moore had decided it was time to go home. He put his punches together with the accuracy and power that distinguishes the artist from the artisan. Poor Pompey, such a gentle guy, showed gameness but there was such a noticeable gap in their fighting class that it became embarrassing to witness. It had taken a great deal of courage for Pompey to leave his corner for the tenth round because his injuries had become severe. Moore clubbed him down three times and there was no chance now that Pompey would be let off the hook. He bravely climbed up each time from the counts of eight, nine and eight, and tried to cover up in a corner. When ref Hart considered that he'd given the challenger every chance to recover, he dived in to halt the massacre.

Moore took his bow and leaned over the ropes to say to old Etonian Onslow Fane, president of the Boxing Board of Control, 'If you're a real Lord you should have my robe,' and the champion presented the garish gown to Fane and left the ring with a towel draped over his shoulders.

Britain could not find another light-heavyweight capable of fighting Moore. I doubt if there ever was a British boxer at Moore's weight who could have extended him except, maybe, the fearless Jock McAvoy, but his best days were at middleweight. Nor would Moore's crablike style have suited swinging Freddie Mills.

Moore's move into the fight game when he was around 15 years old was due chiefly to his colour. In those days boxing was just about the only way a negro could rise above the poverty so many of them were condemned to. His parents separated shortly after his birth and Archie, with sisters Rachel and half-brothers, Louis and Jackie, were brought up in a St Louis slum by uncle Cleveland and Aunt Willie Moore. His uncle died when Archie was four and there was a great deal of affection between him and Auntie.

'We were too poor to paint our home and too proud to whitewash, so we scrubbed everything,' he said, 'It was so clean it was like a hospital.' Poverty, inevitably, brought a brush with the law for Archie and brother, 'Louis was light-fingered by nature, and somehow a man's watch got tangled in his hand, and the man sent the police to ask Louis what time it was.' Archie spent a 22-months term at a Missouri reformatory for somehow acquiring coins from a bus conductor. He regarded the term as his most precious lesson in life. 'I don't say I enjoyed it, but I'm grateful for what it did for me. It gave me a lesson in discipline and they paid me something for the work I did. I should have paid them for what they did for me.'

Much of Moore's retirement time has been devoted to helping youth organisations.

It is doubtful if any boxer matched Moore's dedication to training for his chosen profession. He was a skinny kid who invented methods of developing unusual strength. For example he would walk on his hands completely around a block. His shoulders and biceps he developed by exercising phenomenally on a chinning bar. As a teenager he could chin 355 times. He could also shadow box with one of his Aunt's flat irons in each hand. Six ounce gloves, by comparison, were made of weightless gossamer.

He would shadow box at a mirror and try to teach himself the counters to every punch he aimed. He studied every aspect of boxing. His left-jab was a deadly weapon that softened up many a rival for the kill. It was cunning and cutting.

Yet in 1941, when Moore was probably at his peak, he collapsed in a street and was taken to hospital unconscious. He needed an emergency operation to save his life, he had a perforated ulcer.

The newspaper reports said that even if Archie survived he would not fight again. He was in hospital for 28 days, then during a further convalescent period he had to have another operation for appendicitis. He was, it seemed, a complete physical wreck. Yet he fought all the way back to combat conditions. But a crueller blow was still to come, Moore was ruled out of a fight with a suspected heart murmur when he held the championship. It was the first time anyone could recall seeing Archie utterly defeated. But Doc Kearns (the Doc title was conferred on him by Jack Dempsey, not by the medical profession) decided that Archie's heart condition was correctable.

Specialists continued to diagnose an organic condition, but Moore's persistence finally produced a verdict that the condition was only fibrillation – an irregular heartbeat, correctable by therapy. Only six weeks after a spell of care treatment he fought, and beat, Nino Valdes at a Las Vegas ballpark!

For many years Moore has been respected by his fellow practitioners, but the public at large never gave him complete recognition because he had somehow acquired an unfortunate image – that of the con man who could hit a bit. But any man who could knock Rocky Marciano off his feet must have had something going for him. That blow, in September, 1955, was probably the hardest Archie ever landed in his life. Only Jersey Joe Walcott, a man of the Moore calibre but bigger, had managed to drop the Rock. He came off the floor to defeat both of them, but Moore came within the barest margin of immortality. Marciano's immense strength and threshing machine style punching brought Moore down in nine rounds, but Rocky showed his respect for old Archie's courage and ability by saying, 'Sorry, Arch' as he helped pick the lighter kingpin off the floor. It was Marciano's last fight.

Moore's meeting, for a second crack at the heavyweight championship, now vacant, against Floyd Patterson a year later, is best forgotten. Although Moore subsequently had 31 fights he had lost both fire and ambition that night in Chicago when he met Patterson, then rated the fastest heavy of them all. Moore took the count in round five and wished, as the boxing legend says, he had stayed in bed.

The real transformation of Moore from craftsman to celebrity probably took place 22 years after his first fight when he fought a roughewn Canadian fisherman, Yvon Durelle, in Montreal. It was the early television peak era of boxing and Moore was to earn the respect and affection of the public. They saw his cunning skill and grace, a man of fierce pride and a special kind of valour. He had arrived at the weigh-in wearing a shawl cape and midnight blue dinner jacket, carrying a silver headed cane. 'I am trying to give boxing a touch of class,' he quipped.

But it was the untutored Durelle who came close to proving that clout can overcome class when he put Moore down three times in the first round and once more in the fifth. Yet by the eleventh round of a spectacle as savage as any television viewers had ever seen, Moore came back to crush the Canadian. He did it with a groggy gesture of noblesse obligé.

There was a certain majesty about Moore that night. He had fought largely from instinct climbing off the canvas time after time, finally to take the heart out of a Durelle who wilted in the eleventh. Referee Jack Sharkey, one-time world heavyweight champion, swears that Moore stood over Durelle as Sharkey was completing the ten count and called, 'Please get up, Yvon! I got up for you!'

Inevitably, there was a return bout. Durelle professed that long counts and other vain tricks had cheated him of victory, while Archie chose to speak of revenge only in parables.

He recalled Aesop's fables of the wolf and the lamb, in which the lamb sought with simple logic to establish that he was innocent of any wrong-doing to the wolf and should not, therefore, be eaten. 'I was drinking in the stream,' the wolf snarled (as Archie would quote), 'and you muddied it.' 'But you were drinking from the upstream,' the lamb replied shrewdly. 'Well, I'm about to eat you anyway,' the wolf snapped back.

'So,' said Archie, 'It doesn't matter what Durelle says, I'll eat him anyway,' and he did. The fight was twice post-poned. The first time was because of damage to Archie's right foot – aggravated perhaps by emotional distress at the thought of the food he would have to cut out to make the required 175 lb. The second time was because his wife, Joan (sister of actor Sidney Poitier), was rushed away for an emergency mastoid operation.

Durelle had other problems, too, like getting only 15,000 dollars for a fight that was to pay a fat 175,000 dollars for the champion. By fight time Durelle seemed thoroughly demoralised and was demolished in three rounds.

'They shouldn't enter a mule to race at Santa Anita,' smiled Moore during his post-fight conference.

Moore was a man who could smile after twice being close to death; being on the breadline; in a reformatory; and after four wives, eight managers and nine rounds with Rocky Marciano. Such a man is something special.

8

Ted Kid Lewis

Ted Kid Lewis was arguably the best welterweight this country, or any other country, ever tossed into a ring. He was, unquestionably, the most successful British fighter in American rings. Some contend that Kid Lewis was the greatest pound-for-pound British fighter of all time. I would not contest the argument.

Cradled in the nursery of London's East End Gershon Mendeloff, later to become Ted Kid Lewis, was welterweight champion of the world, British featherweight, welter and middleweight champion. In all, the incomparable Kid won eight undisputed titles and was a claimant to three others.

For almost twenty years the man who had two cauliflower ears adorning a slightly chipped but eminently benevolent head was my guest at the annual Boxing Writers' Club dinner. When he was introduced, usually last among the greats, there was seldom a dry eye in the place. He was a pros pro. And the old Kid usually cried unashamedly.

He died at the Clapham Home for Aged Jews in 1970, taking a secret to his grave. He was, in fact, a year older than recorded in boxing record books. He died at 77, three days short of 78.

It meant that Lewis had won his first British title at 17, twenty-two days before his 18th birthday, and not 16 as reported since that memorable occasion when the East End wonder boy stopped Alec Lambert in 17 rounds for the 9 st. crown in 1912.

Lewis was born at 56, Umberston St, a basement of a gaslit tenement at St Georges-in-the-East within splashing distance of Aldgate pump. The Jews traced their boxing history back to Daniel Mendoza, born in Aldgate, the first Jew to become champion of the world.

The impoverished London district spawned a succession of great fighters, but none matched Lewis, son of a cabinet maker who fled from Russia after witnessing the slaughter of relations.

Ted was a weedy, slightly anaemic child who first had to fight to live, but later lived to fight. One of his brothers died young, another became a modest boxer. His introduction into boxing came with a cobblestone contest with 14-year-old Ted attempting some corrective training against an older boy whom Ted had seen strike a girl. The scrappers were parted and encouraged to finish the argument with gloves on at the local Judean club. Ted agreed, but his rival ducked out. For the prize of sixpence – a penny deducted for tea – scrawny Lewis was beaten by a substitute, Johnny Sharpe, several years his senior, who later became a champion manager.

The Kid changed his name because he feared upsetting his disciplinarian father. He saw the name Harry Lewis, an American fighter, in a *Sporting Life* headline and made the change.

It was the beginning of a 20-year career and 500 battles, some not recorded. The two tickets (trade term for cauliflower ears) were received in meaningless bouts, winning a 9 st. novices competition and later boxing a charity exhibition on stage at the Kilburn Empire. But Ted told me he never recalled having a cut-eye, the curse of modern boxing, in his entire career. The first ear swelling was the cause of the Kid deciding to leave home, when his mother almost passed out at the sight of her pale faced son in apparent pain. He paid fivepence a night at Fusco's lodging house, sharing it with other East End scrappers Alf Mansfield, Young Brooks and Jackie Phillips.

He sold newspapers at the corner of Commercial Road and Cannon Street. But fighting was to be his profession. He actually liked the game, and he was totally devoid of fear. At the peak of his career Lewis never weighed more than 10 st., yet he sparred with mighty Jack Johnson and Jack Dempsey and was not invited back.

In these pinchbeck days when boxers or managers argue over ounces it seems incredible that he conceded alarming amounts of weight. For example, 10 st. Lewis defeated the reigning light-heavyweight (12 st. 7 lb.) champion of Britain. It is almost impossible to imagine just how great Lewis was.

He was the forerunner of the current flashy, combination punching style. Many of the fighters of the Lewis era were mechanical and predictable. They called them deliberate hitters. Lewis carried his arms low (against text book teachings) and fought with his mouth open (to horrify boxing instructors). His punches usually landed in clusters.

He fashioned the gumshield, or mouthpiece, because he had jagged front teeth that threatened to protrude through his lip when hit solidly. A dentist friend, Jack Marks, made the gumshield for him and Marks was credited with being the inventor. I discussed the making of the first shield with Mr Marks who practised at Notting Hill. It was made of gutta-percha, a dental substance for taking an impression to make dentures.

Lewis's insistence on wearing a gumshield brought numerous rows during his remarkable five years fighting in the United States. It was later universally accepted, and medically recommended, though a gumshield is not obligatory. It is the only protection permitted above the waistline.

The early Lewis years were up and down in every aspect. At 16, he was earning fifty-shillings a fight and sending it home to his mother. He made the mistake of forgetting to

duck against Duke Lynch and was k.o.'d for the only in-
disputable time in his career – a contest not recorded in all
record books. But Lewis also twice whacked Lynch who
never made the big-time.

In the period from 1909 to Christmas Eve 1911 Lewis
had 58 recorded fights, and a few that were lost by the com-
pilers. Most of them were at the Judean Club and then the
famous Blackfriars Ring. He lost only four.

There was a spiteful, cold-blooded attitude of fighting by
Lewis that suggested the world owed him and his family a
living. He was bold and relentless. A world beater from the
start.

He swaggered and spent money recklessly – but usually on
others. He grew to live at the rate of a thousand pounds a
week, loved gambling, diamonds, furs and fast cars.

Lewis's heart was even bigger outside the ring because he
was an 'easy touch' for a hard luck story and he roamed the
streets of Whitechapel showering silver coins like confetti to
poor kids. He paid for regular trips to the sea for hordes of
East End kids. Some rose to become wealthy men and I
frequently saw them doff their hats to the idol who had been
like a godfather.

Lewis had the magnetism of a Muhammad Ali among his
own people. He was worshipped. Like Ali, Lewis did not
believe in false modesty. He never saw a boxer he did not
believe he could beat.

At 17, Lewis fought twenty-rounders. Four months after
defeating Lambert for the featherweight title, he took the
European crown from Paul Til, of France, who was disqualified for persistent holding. The boy Lewis had frightened
the champion.

In 1914, a month after winning his second title, Lewis
began his globe trotting. He went to Australia, knocking out
a 12 st. stoker who had persistently challenged him during
training on the voyage. Six weeks at sea ended with a party
and Lewis was asked to fight Herb McCoy, the Aussie cham-

E

pion with only twelve hours notice. He obliged and won a 20-round decision at Sydney.

Sir Harry Lauder, entertaining in Australia, sent the Kid a congratulation telegram. He had struck a sporting blow for home. There were four more fights Down Under, including a losing, though disputed, verdict in a return against McCoy in Melbourne.

The Americans soon heard about the brash Londoner who feared no man, and who could box like a ballet dancer or battle like a demon. He was asked to join Charlie Harvey, a manager of repute, in the States. Lewis left Australia with another 20-round win over Bobby Moore and landed at San Francisco only to be played for a sucker by card sharps on the four days and nights Sante Fe train trip to New York. Gambling was Lewis's weakness but he resented being conned like a country boy and managed to 'persuade' the offending sharpers to return his cash.

Charlie Harvey was the then New York Athletic Commission chief and he could not officially act as Ted's manager. Jimmy Johnston, later to be known on the boxing beat as the Boy Bandit, was Harvey's office worker and was to look after the Limey.

Lewis wore out, hired and fired managers, like many football clubs. He set a high standard for himself and expected a manager to be the same. The Kid could speak for himself. He was restless, like most champions, and had fire in his belly.

Lewis was a go-getter who chatted like Ali and taunted many opponents. He was not the film caster's idea of a shy Englishman. Lewis could also back up his boasts.

But Lewis's partnership in America with Harvey compared with the modern Henry Cooper/Jim Wicks association. Lewis liked Harvey and they never bothered to sign a contract. Both were men of their word.

Harvey launched his find from his offices at 1402 Broadway and Lewis trained at Dai Hawkins' roadhouse at

Westchester, NY where Jess Willard and Bombardier Billy Wells had worked.

Lewis learned to adapt his style from flash and tricky to the accepted walk-in American type. If the going got too tough – and Lewis regularly conceded weight – he reverted to the cuter technique which came naturally to him. But for most of his career Lewis was a slugger.

The American grapevine learned of Lewis's prowess and it was some time before Harvey could find an opponent. Lewis had beaten Young Joe Shugrue, one of America's best lightweights, during his Australian campaign, and the fight traders were wary. Eventually, Lewis was matched with Phil Bloom at Madison Square Garden – a fight shrine to the cockney. In 1914 boxing was outlawed in every State except Louisiana, and though promotions were permitted, no decisions were rendered. It was a way of beating the State law and presenting an exhibition. The newspaper critics awarded decisions and many of Lewis's fights are registered as ND – newspaper decision.

Bat Masterson, the wild west sheriff, was also a New York sportswriter who gave Lewis his first review and awarded him the decision over Bloom. It was the start of a campaign that struck fear into the hearts of many an American fighter and Lewis did more than any other Briton (though he was later aided by another all-action East Ender, Jack Kid Berg) to dispel the American joke about Britons being horizontal champs.

Lewis fought with fractured hands and in stockinged feet when he was broke. He hobnobbed with racketeers and royalty, knew Winston Churchill, loved life, spent freely, had a long happy marriage to an American, Elsie, and passed away within hours of winning a hand at cards.

The big money began to come for Lewis when he was promised 5,000 dollars to fight Frankie Mack in Cuba, where decisions were permitted, a month before the Jack Johnson *v.* Jess Willard heavyweight match, in 1915.

It took Lewis four days by boat to reach Havana where he was part of a circus tour. He defeated Mack over 20 rounds and was paid in silver dollars thrown into a hat which was later counted as 2,000 dollars.

'Somebody had dipped into the hat before I got to the dressing room,' said Lewis.

He trained and ran with the controversial Johnson whom Lewis rated the greatest heavyweight of all.

In March 1915 Lewis was back on the New York circuit and matched with Jack Britton – the first of a record series of twenty fights in twelve U.S. cities.

Britton (real name William J. Breslin) was obviously ideally styled to give Lewis an even fight. He was nine years older than Lewis and had a pro career stretching 26 years. He lost only 24 times. When Britton first fought Lewis he had lost only six of 141 fights.

The second Britton *v.* Lewis match at Boston in August 1915 is recorded in *Ring* record book and generally accepted as for the world welterweight title. Lewis won a 12-rounds decision, and repeated the win a month later in Boston.

To set the record straight Lewis did not officially win the welterweight crown until being awarded the newspaper verdict over Willie Ritchie in New York, December 28, 1915.

Though Lewis was a developing welter he could scale down to lightweight at 9 st. 9 lb. (135 lb.) and his advisers insisted upon the first match with Britton being at lightweight. The ploy was to force Britton to be weight-drained and by Lewis winning it would tempt a showdown fight with Freddy Welsh, the great Welshman who was the world 9 st. 9 lb. champion but who was not interested in fighting either Lewis or Britton.

Lewis 'made' the exact lightweight poundage in Boston, but Britton weighed fully clothed and said he had not agreed to scale below welterweight limit.

It was the first of many rows between Britton's manager, Dumb Dan Morgan, who never stopped talking, and perky

Jimmy Johnston who had taken over from Harvey. Morgan forced referee Pat Haley to unwind Lewis's hand bandages and check for hidden horsehoes, but when the opening bell rang Britton refused to come out fighting until Lewis was made to dispense with his gumshield which, at the time, had not been condoned by boxing commissions.

But Lewis was not rattled by the gamesmanship; though being unable to keep Britton down he was able to gain the majority newspaper vote in the two fights regarded by some as for the title.

Willie Ritchie had been lightweight champion but outgrew the division and moved to welterweight, although Lewis weighed just under 10 st., he was good enough to whip the wildcat. Lewis was credited with eight of ten rounds in every ringside report and heralded as world champion. Lewis rated Ritchie, later to become a State Commission chairman, as a great and sporting fighter. It was an achievement for Lewis to defeat him.

During 1915 Lewis yearned for his first visit home and had booked a passage on the Lusitania. He cancelled to take a fight in Montreal when the ship was torpedoed off the Irish Coast.

Winning against Ritchie had completed 232 rounds in thirteen months, but the Kid preferred fighting to training. Only four days after becoming champion Lewis fought ten rounds against Kayo Brennan in Buffalo.

In April 1916 Lewis fought Britton a sixth time in New Orleans where decisions were allowed and Lewis lost his world crown with a 20-round points decision.

There was good pickings for Lewis during his title reign. Backers of highly-rated Jimmy Duffy laid 1,000 to 250 dollars that their man could defeat the champion. Lewis insisted on the cash being deposited in a hotel safe before he yawned and knocked out Duffy in 1 min. 40 secs.

Lewis's desire for action was alarming by any era. During 1916 he fought 42 rounds against four opponents – including

Britton – in 21 days! He accepted the skilful Britton as a substitute for a less formidable opponent who had cried off.

The kid sent for his parents, two brothers and three sisters, to stay with him in America and earned the fare money by fighting six times in 25 days and winning a fight where he conceded 16 lbs.

The fights with Britton, totalling 222 rounds, took their toll, Lewis's hands were buckled and puffed and resembled cobra heads. Britton was a cagey performer who blocked blows with his forearms and elbows and Lewis damaged his hands trying to break through Britton's defence.

When they met for the twentieth time it seemed the moves had been choreographed. Yet their fights never failed to please. They never slacked. 'Zie Clig,' Lewis's trainer, Zalie Goodman, would yell. It means 'Be clever' in Yiddish. But Britton understood the call and matched Lewis for wits.

Lewis won three contests; Britton five, with one drawn and eleven no-decision bouts. They fought three times in nineteen days!

The tag Crashing, Bashing, Dashing Ted Kid Lewis was spread across the American headlines. He was a ruthless fighting machine.

Lewis conceded $9\frac{1}{2}$ lb. against near middleweight Mike Gibbons, a star performer, who said he preferred to take on heavies than lights like Lewis. A week later Lewis won in Dayton, Ohio.

The master match was Lewis, who lost and regained the welterweight crown, against Benny Leonard, the lightweight champion classed as a master. They fought at the Newark (New Jersey) International Ball Park in 1918 when both were lodging in Harlem.

Leonard was a PT instuctor and Lewis had served in the U.S. Army at Atlanta, Georgia, under the wing of old rival Mike Gibbons. He was stricken with yellow jaundice when the World War One armistice was signed.

Leonard made many stipulations before agreeing to meet

Lewis, including his own choice of referee and having his chief second standing in Lewis's corner. The fighters became artful dodgers, feinting and clutching, both becoming a show off for an eight-rounder that was publicised as a fight-to-the-finish bareknuckle brawl.

It was one of Lewis's most disappointing fights. The morning editions voted in his favour and the evening papers leaned towards Leonard. Nobody argued with a draw.

Lewis's homecoming was timely – a fight against an old friend and foe, Matt Wells, on Boxing Day 1919, at the Royal Albert Hall. Critics here reckoned the U.S. circuit had burned the Kid out. He had fought and beaten the best.

But, at 25, Lewis was unstoppable. He pounded the clever Wells, British lightweight champion, for twelve rounds, and when the referee stopped the fight calling 'That's sufficient' it was Wells who quipped, 'I've been trying to think of that word for the last twelve rounds!'

Four more knockouts and Lewis was back in the title business. He had no trouble knocking out Johnny Bee in four rounds to become British middleweight champion – the 11 st. 6 lb. division. Then came the first of four memorable clashes with Johnny Basham, of Newport, Mon, known as the Happy Warrior and a particular favourite of my grandfather, Arthur, who seconded both Basham and Lewis.

They gave Basham, the ex-Welsh fusilier, £5,000 to put up the British, Empire and European welterweight titles against Lewis at Olympia, London, on June 9, 1920. Basham, a superb boxer, staved the sphinx-like Lewis off at the start but the threshing machine caught up with him by the ninth round. Basham was bleeding heavily from the mouth (he refused to wear a gumshield) and was stopped when his right ear ballooned.

Lewis fought Basham four times with Lewis winning each time, the last bout was in 1929 – nine years after their first championship clash – when both were old as boxers go. The match of the old gentlemen was relegated to Hoxton Baths in London for a show not licensed by the British Board of Control which was formed that year.

Lewis, of course, won in three rounds. It was the old Kid's last fight at 35.

The Lewis-Basham series, lasting nine, nineteen, twelve and three-rounds are a hallowed section of British fight history. They were ruthless yet sporting.

But it is difficult to highlight any particular Lewis fight when all, in their way, were radiant. There was the 1921 match against Jack Bloomfield for the middleweight crown that was so big the promoting National Sporting Club, who virtually ruled the game, had to take a contest outside their Covent Garden premises for the first time. Holland Park rink was hired for Lewis, weighing 10 st. 5 lb. in his underwear, to defeat Bloomfield, who scaled a fraction inside 11 st. 6 lb. As a recent comparison, world welterweight champion, Jose Napoles, found it an impossible task against the middleweight champion, Carlos Monzon, in Paris during 1974.

Lewis completely wrecked the boxing adage that a good big 'un always beats a good little 'un.

Lewis weighed 11 st. 6 lb., his heaviest, to knock out Tom Gummer a leading heavyweight at 13 st. 10 lb. in the first round.

Knocking out Gummer clinched Lewis's biggest and most controversial fight. Georges Carpentier, the idol of France, light-heavyweight champion of the world, was among the audience at the Dome, Brighton, and Lewis had dressed hurriedly before they fully revived the luckless Gummer to march straight up to Carpentier and call, 'Why won't you fight me?'

Carpentier, acutely conscious of the newsmen around him, paused and then replied, 'You find somebody to stage it and I'll fight you.'

Within a week Major Arnold Wilson, then London's No. 1 promoter, signed articles and moved from his regular venue, the Royal Albert Hall, to book the London Olympia. Receipts reached an indoor record of £43,000 with Carpentier getting £15,000 and Lewis £12,000.

The fight, with ringside seats a record twenty-five guineas, was for Carpentier's European heavyweight crown. Lewis struck training camp at Harrow-on-the-Hill where the followers included Sir Harry Lauder, Sophie Tucker and the Marx Brothers.

The excitement of the fight matched any in British history. Very pistol lights, coloured green for victory, red for defeat, were to be fired outside the Olympia to announce the result to anxious Londoners.

Squads of police were called to control the crowds for the mere weigh-in ceremony, held at Blackfriars Ring, when a fully dressed Lewis scaled 10 st. 12 lb. and Carpentier scaled the exact light-heavy poundage of 12 st. 7 lb.

Lewis clambered into the ring for his customary parade that included leaning through the ropes to shake hands with bowler-hatted toffs and wave to his pals further back. The Kid was a forerunner of the Ali technique.

The Duke of York, Prince George (later the Duke of Kent), and world champion, Jack Dempsey, arrived at the ringside while the contestants were read the customary police warning about their responsibility in the event of a fatality.

Carpentier's manager, Francois Descamps, noisily objected to Lewis wearing a gumshield and was roundly booed. When the opening bell sounded the smile left Lewis's face. He never went into a fight with more spite in his heart.

There was no preliminary sparring and Carpentier, with a 23 lb. advantage and four inches of height in his favour, proffered some tentative left leads to keep Lewis at bay. But the Kid was too wise and skilfully slipped inside the lead to plant a venomous right-hand on the Frenchman's jaw.

Carpentier instinctively grabbed Lewis's arm and hooked a right under his heart. Lewis wrenched fiercely at the enfolding armlock and London referee, Joe Palmer, moved in to separate them.

They broke and Lewis was mumbling his disapproval at the bigger man's tactics and, at the same time, hurled himself back into battle. Lewis was getting the inside position and a trickle of blood came from Carpentier's mouth.

Again the fighters clinched, with Lewis trying to hook hard 'downstairs' and neither would give ground. They broke at Palmer's stern behest but Carpentier uppercutted Lewis as they parted. Until the sixties British boxing permitted hitting on the break with a 'defend yourself at all times' warning.

Carpentier and Lewis glared angrily at each other as the Frenchman tried to nullify Lewis's aggression by clutching. 'Stop!', cried the referee, 'This clinching must stop'.

Lewis lowered his arms and turned his head to protest his innocence . . . and for one split second took his eyes off his opponent. I have seen the film view a dozen times. Palmer was admonishing Lewis and also touching his wrist.

Carpentier, a finisher second to none, decided to take advantage of this open target – and, maybe, apologise later. He teed-off a right, straight as a dart, to Lewis's defenceless jaw – the knock-out point.

Lewis crumpled like a sack and stayed on his knees from one to out – to the tune of thunderous protest. 'Not until Carpentier helped me up and they started sponging my face did I realise what had happened,' said Lewis.

Lord Lonsdale led the contemporary opinion that Lewis had been cheated. The whole country was in an uproar. 'Defend yourself at all times' was the cardinal precept of boxing, but did this include the period when a referee had ordered a ceasefire?

Joe Palmer did not officiate for another big fight. Lewis repeatedly challenged Carpentier to a return but the handsome Georges got himself chopped to pieces against Battling Siki, losing his world title, and was not interested in fighting Lewis again.

I hosted an occasion when the old timers met, both in their seventies. 'I don't bear any grudge now,' said Lewis, 'But I still think you took a bit of liberty, George.'

Carpentier, gravel voiced, replied, 'But Kid, the referee never said, "Stop Boxing". I was perfectly in order to carry on.'

Because the referee was touching Lewis at the time there is no doubt in my mind that Carpentier should have been disqualified. Or was it Lewis's fault for arguing? It will always remain an open verdict.

But nobody could keep Lewis down for long. A month later he was defending the British Empire middleweight title against Frankie Burns. He had collected *six* championships and a Lonsdale Belt within two years. To celebrate Lewis paid for 1,000 poor children to visit the seaside for the day.

There was a second meeting between Lewis, the star of the East End, and Augie Ratner, the hero of the New York East Side. 'Full of hate, that one was,' says promoter Harry Levene who handled Ratner here.

Lewis dropped, once again, from middleweight to welter and fractured a hand fighting Scot Tommy Milligan in Edinburgh. Lewis lost three titles in a twenty-rounder. 1925 was the start of the Lewis decline, losing three of six fights by disqualification. 'Those guys didn't know what rough fighting was all about. They'd have laughed at them in America,' said Lewis.

His final fling came with a last visit to America in 1928 where Lewis lost, again by disqualification, to Maxie (Slapsie) Rosenbloom who had held the world light-heavyweight championship. 'I was thrown out for hitting too hard!' quipped Lewis.

On the way home Lewis dropped off in Canada to concede two-and-a-half stone to world class heavyweight, Charlie Belanger, but Lewis retired hurt in the first round. It was a rare flop.

Lewis frequently told me that the fight he remembered

most and which was, perhaps, his hardest was a mere four-rounder – a draw – against Mexican Battling Ortega in Oakland, California, on October 24, 1917.

California law forbid contests of longer duration and Lewis thought nothing of conceding a mere 20 lb. to a rugged battler determined to make his mark against the then world champion.

Lewis could not understand why he struggled and was forced to hit, run and finally hold against an opponent whom he had reckoned he could defeat with one hand tied behind his back. He felt almost lifeless and admitted being relieved, and lucky, to walk out with a draw.

A few hours later a telegram was delivered to Lewis announcing that a son had weighed-in at seven pounds in New York. Morton, to be Ted's only child, was born while the champ was in the ring. It was the champ's only explanation for having suddenly, and inexplicably, been drained of his strength.

During a subsequent trip to South Africa, Lewis bought Morton (his godfather is Charlie Chaplin) a Brownie camera. Some say it was the best buy of Lewis's life. His son later worked in Hollywood and became a film producer. Morton Lewis's London company produced the 1970 and 1974 world cup soccer film.

It was Morton who cared for the champ in his waning years. Old Ted virtually quit in his corner, for the first time in his life, when his wife died. He also suffered from Parkinson Disease.

Only four years before his death Lewis was awarded a silver ring engraved : 'The best old boxer of this year – and any other year,' by the Boxing Writers' Club. For the first time in his life the Kid was speechless and he cried with pride. He was the Golden Oldie.

Lewis contended that he had lived on borrowed time since he climbed out of a ring, for the last time, in 1929. He was a natural fighter – and nothing else. He tried being a manager; a referee (handling Vince Dundee *v.* Jack Hood); selling shirts; a travel agent; security officer; and endless other jobs.

'I reckon I'd still be welterweight champion of the world if that lucky so-and-so Britton hadn't beaten me when I was suffering the effects of typhoid fever,' he said.

At Lewis's funeral service at an East Ham synagogue Rev. M. Woolf said, 'He was respected all his life by Jew and Gentile alike. When he had money he gave it to the poor.'

£250,000 had come and gone but Ted Kid Lewis had his memories – and a million admirers. I am honoured to have been among his many friends.

9
Jimmy Wilde

Wherever men fight, and wherever men talk of boxing, the pallid little Welsh collier, Jimmy Wilde, is established as a legend-beyond the mists of memory, beyond the rust of time.

During the Olympic Games in Mexico, 1968, four British writer-commentators, Peter Wilson, Harry Carpenter, George Whiting and myself were asked to judge 'the greatest ever' to decide a competition.

We debated loud and long until none of us could find a fault with the nomination of flyweight Wilde. He is the only non-American to be rated No. 1 in the all-time great list of *Ring* magazine, ranked in the Hall of Fame in 1959 – forty-six years after his last fight.

The 1968 honour was to be Wilde's final accolade. Six months later he died, at 76, at Whitchurch Hospital, Cardiff, where he had been a patient for four years.

Six weeks before his death I visited Wilde in the public Tegfan Ward where the elderly were tended, many, like Wilde, were suffering from senility. He was not bed-ridden and his body had the sheen of a new-born baby. His blue eyes glowed and he smiled at everyone.

But little Jimmy's memory had gone and he was not even aware that his wife, Elizabeth, had passed away two years earlier. They had wed as teenagers.

Inevitably, the boxing knockers would have us believe that the years of taking punishment, – an unofficial career of 864 bouts from fairground booth to big arena – with only *four* losses –, had finally robbed the little man of his senses. Truth was Wilde never fully recovered from a serious car accident at Cadoxton, Glamorgan, only a few years earlier. He was also brutally beaten-up by a gang of thugs on a lonely railway station in Wales.

There were wealthy businessmen, even a professor, sharing the Whitchurch ward with Wilde who were suffering from a similar complaint, and none of them had ever stepped into a prize ring.

Although they buried Wilde, who weighed less than a sack of coal, at Barry on March 14, 1969, his masculinity is still alive among the miners who worshipped him.

The freakish wizardry of his knuckles is imperishable. Had Jimmy Wilde been fighting a half a century later he would have made half a million, been publicised as a phenomenon, televised ad nauseam, and possibly knighted.

Yet at his peak Wilde weighed 6 st. 10 lb.! He stood 5 ft. 2½ in., took the world flyweight championship from the Zulu Kid (real name Guiseppe Di Melfi) in 1916 and held it until losing to Pancho Villa in New York seven years later. It was Wilde's last fight.

Wilde had nine world or British title fights and Tancy Lee was the only Briton to defeat him in a sketchy record of 140 fights, of which he won 77 on knockouts or stoppages, 48 on points and one on a foul. He drew two, had eight no-decision bouts in the States, was outpointed once and stopped three times.

The defeat by Lee, when Wilde was suffering from 'flu, was later avenged with the Welshman stopping the Scot in eleven rounds.

Wilde had licked all-comers from the 8 st, to 9 st., divisions, where weight conceding is a mighty handicap, in anything from one to twenty rounds. In his 'fight all-comers' days on the boxing booths he once performed the incredible feat of knocking over 23 opponents inside four hours, and all with the frame of a gnat. Weight rules were not observed in the booths of the hungry early years of this century, and Wilde was expected to concede two stone to any challenger who sought a pound by staying the regulation three rounds with the anaemic looking miner. For his day's work Wilde received thirty-shillings.

He was hailed the Tylorstown Terror, the Ghost with a Hammer in his Hand, the Indian Famine, the Mighty Atom, and a dozen other endearments. He was an Oliver Twist who dished out plenty.

Wilde was managed by Teddy Lewis who often cunningly contrived that important opponents had to stew themselves on the scales which meant Wilde was odds-on to chop them up quickly. My grandfather, Arthur, who seconded Wilde on several occasions, was so steeped in boxing orthodoxy that he could never fathom whether Wilde was genius or freak. Certainly there is a sound argument that Scot Benny Lynch, flyweight hero of the thirties, was an equal if not superior to Wilde, but no little man matched Wilde's achievements.

Imagine a man with these statistics being able to strike fear into the hearts of hardened, heavier fighters. Reach: 66 in., chest: $31\frac{3}{4}$ in., waist: $25\frac{3}{4}$ in., thigh: 21 in., wrist: $6\frac{1}{4}$ in., biceps: $11\frac{1}{2}$ in. He often weighed-in fully clothed, wearing a bowler hat, and carrying lead in his pockets because some American States barred matches of unequal weights.

Born at Quakers Yard, Rhondda Valley, – I have made the pilgrimage to see the now broken cottage birthplace of the great one – Jimmy Wilde began his amazing scrap saga at 18, having married the daughter of a boxer, and fathered a son, David, who was to have a brief pro career during the thirties.

With the South Wales pits idle, he demanded a fight at the Millfield Athletic Club. Derided by doorkeepers, laughed at by ringside experts, the importunate waif pasted his opponent and bought his wife half-a-pound of chocolate almonds from the five-shillings purse.

At 20, Wilde argued his way into the London Blackfriars Ring, where it appears the Cockney management were reluctant to expose so fragile a youth to the ribaldry of the Sunday afternoon crowd and to the well advertised punches of Young Nipper. Jimmy knocked him out in 45 seconds.

The Welshman had never had a boxing lesson in his life though he sparred with Dai Davies, his father-in-law who fought professionally. Dai's daughter had pleaded with Jimmy to abandon ideas of fighting for money if they were to be married and others warned Jimmy that he did not have the strength to survive the punishing life of a fighter. But Wilde was a sawn-off Muhammad Ali who would have fought Jack Johnson if they provided the stilts for Jimmy to reach his jaw. He had no occupational fears.

His wife decided that if Jimmy could not be persuaded to lay down the gloves she would at least make sure he was fully prepared. She often cycled to accompany Jimmy on his training runs. For fifteen years the champion-to-be rarely missed a day's training, and when Wilde was unable to secure sparmates it was Elizabeth-Ann who donned the gloves and provided a target for her husband! An idyll, that marriage. But Wilde was to repay his wife a thousand times for her devotion. She later wore a collar of diamonds that Wilde had accepted as a purse for a fight.

Wilde's aptitude for boxing was natural. His punching was not heavy or crushing but was sharp, sudden, and usually directed at the exact spot where the blows would be most effective. Jimmy knew nothing of anatomy but an anatomist, working with calipers and chart could not have picked vital spots as neatly as Wilde who, in a flash of inspiration, could pick the spot and plant his steel-hammer fist bang on it.

Wilde had a natural talent for being able to box without tension in his body, yet be able to explode his pipe-stem arms at a furious rate when he was ready to finish a rival. He was like an octopus. The punches rained from all angles.

Sometimes Wilde could be a one-punch wrecker but, generally, it was the speed of Wilde's blows that confused, and usually downed, opponents. His years of boxing booth training taught Wilde how to cope with unorthodox attacks and he was able to 'read' an opponent's moves. His anticipation was uncanny.

From 1911 until 1914 there is no record of a Wilde defeat and he won the British 8 st. title by outpointing Joe Symonds at the National Sporting Club on November 16, 1914, having previously beaten Londoner Sid Smith, the first holder of the division formed in 1911. It was Wilde's 89th successive victory, following a recorded draw in 1911 against George Luke. Two months later Wilde was beaten for the first time, losing both British and European championships to Tancy Lee in seventeen rounds.

Losing to Lee rankled with Wilde because he came from a sickbed after being plagued with 'flu for three weeks. His illness was an open secret in Wales and, no doubt, Lee, a formidable fighter, had heard the word. Lee put the pressure on Wilde and it says much for the champion's courage that he lasted until the seventeenth round.

Wilde's ear ballooned into a painful cauliflower and his seconds worked frantically to staunch the cuts on his face. My grandfather was among those seconds and it was he who handed manager Lewis a blood-stained towel to throw into the ring as a surrender token when poor Wilde was stumbling pathetically.

Wilde was angry and struggled to kick the towel out and argued with his manager, 'Never throw the towel in. If the other fellow can put me down and out, let him have the credit for it.'

Honour had to wait fifteen months before a fully fit Wilde, having already regained the titles from Symonds, who had dethroned Lee, defended them against Lee. This time it was Wilde the winner in eleven rounds.

During the height of the First World War, Wilde became world champion by knocking-out America's Young Zulu Kid, a white man of Italian stock, in eleven rounds at Holborn Stadium. Wilde's fights with Symonds, Lee, Johnny Rosner and Johnny Hughes, were recognised as world title matches in Britain, but the defeat of Zulu Kid gave Wilde universal acclaim.

Wilde, unlike many champions, was not reckless with his cash. He was thrifty. Some American writers chided him for meanness, but Wilde was determined not to go back to the breadline again.

During the war, when Wilde weighed 7 st. 6 lb. wearing his Army greatcoat as a company sergeant major, he was matched with stiff hitting featherweight, Joe Conn, at Chelsea football ground. Because he was a serving soldier Wilde was not permitted to accept pay. Promoter Jack Callaghan paid Wilde in diamonds and Conn, a fine craftsman, was beaten in twelve rounds.

To make yet another modern comparison it was like Walter McGowan, the dancing Scot eight-stoner, being able to stop Howard Winstone, the featherweight champion from Wales.

Whether or not the boiling down process took the steam out of Conn is another story. Wilde's manager was entitled to try any ploy to give his midget an advantage.

Wilde's fight against Pete Herman, Brooklyn-born Pietro Gulotta, former bantamweight champion of the world, is etched in boxing history. It is catalogued as the fight Wilde fought only to please the Prince of Wales.

On January 13, 1921, five years after winning the world title, Wilde, approaching his 29th birthday, was paid £8,000, plus £250 expenses – colossal money for that time – to fight Yank Herman for the 8 st. 6 lb. crown.

Herman's share for the fight at the Royal Albert Hall was undisclosed but referee Jack Smith was guaranteed £50 in £1 notes. No sooner had the signatures been dried than a stroke was pulled in New York. Herman happened to lose his world crown against fellow American, Joe Lynch, the night before he sailed to England. (This was not the Joe Lynch whom Wilde had twice beaten.)

This stratagem took care of little Jimmy's bantamweight aspirations.

It was the start of a pre-fight shambles with Herman now titleless, and his compatriot, Battling Levinsky, the ex-light-heavy champion, withdrawing from a supporting bout against Bombardier Billy Wells because of a dislocated shoulder.

Some of the Royal Albert Hall customers, upset by badly sited ring lights, began scrambling for a better view and Master of Ceremonies, Ron Adair, threatened to pack up and go home.

Then came another Herman bombshell. Brandishing a contract the American refused, point-blank, to weigh-in at ringside. Herman's piece of paper decreed he may weigh at two o'clock on the day of the fight. Herman fulfilled his contract, scaled inside the limit of 8 st. 6 lb., and then ate a hearty meal. He could not have weighed less at fight time. It was a cock-eyed set up because Wilde, having been side-tracked out of an earlier contract to fight Herman, had gone to America, cleaned up, and arrived home considering retirement in a new house built at Cardiff. An American actor, Rube Welch, had tempted Wilde back with the £8,000 purse.

Officials tried to sort out the confusion while Wilde, understandably angry at what he considered another dose of double dealing, refused to budge from his dressing room. Wilde weighed 7 st. 1 lb. Herman was not an ounce lighter than 8 st. 8 lb.

Pleas, promises, solicitations, threats, all were going on backstage. But neither side would budge. Then a red-faced gent entered Wilde's dressing room with the news that the Prince of Wales was waiting for the fight to begin and that his companion, Lord Lonsdale, was on his way to talk to the frustrated Wilde.

Wilde, fretful and fuming, cried : 'I'm tired of all these arguments. I don't care what Herman weighs. If the Prince of Wales wants me to fight, I'll fight.'

Ten minutes later the Prince was mounting the ring apron, thanking Wilde and asking, 'Do you think you can beat Herman?' 'No, Sir,' replied Wilde, 'Not after all this bother. But he'll have to knock me senseless to beat me.'

With 20 lbs. advantage Herman, tradesman of high rating, encouraged angry Wilde to fling his wiry frame at him and drain the sap from his matchstick legs. Herman had a wonderful pair of shoulders for a small man and his speciality was body hitting and durability. He could outlast and outpunch most opponents.

Yet Herman had won the world title from Dane Kid Williams with only one good eye in 1917 and five years later, after many fruitless examinations by specialists, Herman retired to become a club owner in New Orleans. He spent the last forty years of his life totally blind.

Herman's size gave him complete superiority over Wilde. It was a meaningless match that was taken for the money. And it proved painful for Wilde – a contributory cause of him later losing his world crown.

By the ninth round Wilde's famed left was lowering to half mast; by the twelfth his reserves were spent. Herman stayed in pursuit of the wisp who wore a black jockstrap above a thigh lengthened pair of woollen bathing trunks. There was nothing extrovert about Wilde. He did not dress up for royalty.

By round seventeen Wilde was coming apart at the seams. It was a miracle that he had resisted being knocked out. Then Herman triggered the straightest of short rights at Wilde's unprotected chin which pitched the shocked Welshman almost out of the ring. He rose at the count of seven trying to control disobedient legs and this time Herman unloaded a venomous right-hander that sent Wilde bundling into the ropes like a rag doll. Again the brave Wilde, having cracked his head on the ring apron, tried to haul himself up when lesser men would have stayed down.

Wilde, aware of his promise to the Prince, tottered back at the nine-count and swayed pathetically towards the comparatively fresh Herman who was prepared to finish his execution. But Wilde, at least, was spared the indignity of a count out. Referee Smith, in evening dress complete with waistcoat and chain, gathered Wilde in his arms and waved the American aside.

'I'm sorry Jimmy,' he said, 'I have to pick you up because you don't know how to lie down.'

Herman was never given complete credit for his victory because he had antagonised the crowd by not weighing-in at ringside. He is alleged to have later been hit where it hurts most – in the pocket. He did not collect the whole of the money he alleged having been promised.

Six months later Herman came back to fight a bantamweight, Jim Higgins, at the National Sporting Club. He won by a k.o. in eleven rounds. But Herman was overweight again. We can take it for granted that he did manage to scale the correct weight for the formality of regaining the world crown from old pal Lynch in New York seven months after beating Wilde.

The beating was to leave a mark on Wilde. For two years Wilde rested. He was old fistically. Past his prime, but refusing to believe he was washed up. It is not easy for a champion to hand back his crown without reward and Wilde could not refuse the bait of £13,000 – a fantastic sum for the era – to defend his world title against a fiery Filipino who called himself Pancho Villa. Wilde was 31 and Villa ten years younger. They met on a humid June night in 1923 at the Polo Grounds, New York, where many years later I suffered in near-fainting humidity without even having to throw a punch. Just reporting a world heavyweight championship within the glare of the ring arc lights on a breathless night is an unforgettable experience.

Villa was a perfectly proportioned flyweight and a roar went up when the challenger ducked through the ropes wearing a black Japanese kimono. Wilde, looking paler than ever, did not fear Villa or the occasion. Friends and manager Lewis, knew that Wilde was hitting the boxing slide but Jimmy believed in himself until the end.

The champion threw himself into battle with the exuberance of a kid having his first playground scrap, but the lead had begun to show in Wilde's legs.

Villa was a purposeful puncher and by being aggressive the challenger was able to brush aside many of Wilde's darting attacks. But Wilde's spirit turned the fight into a classic. Villa's blows were spiteful and cutting and Wilde's face, showing added scar tissue after the Herman hammering, was being split.

In the sixth Villa sensed that he was facing a champion who was ripe for the picking and poker faced Pancho increased the volume of his attacks. Villa favoured a right-cross and having sighted Wilde's chin he waited for the right moment to unleash a blow capable of flooring a man twice the weight and size of Wilde. Wilde's eyes rolled in disbelief and he crumbled to the canvas. Before touchdown the bell rang and Villa was deprived of the chance to follow up had Wilde been able to get up. Not until the Sixties was it universally recognised that a bell could not interrupt a count, except at the end of the final round.

Under present day rulings Wilde may well have been counted out between the sixth and seventh rounds, but the Welshman's seconds were able to drag him back to the safety of a corner stool and douse him with water. This practice has since been ruled out of order.

Wilde, in a repeat of his fight with Herman, revived sufficiently to argue that he would not be retired in his corner. It is my firm belief that a chief second should not accept a bemused boxer's brave plea to be allowed to 'come out for more' and should make the gesture of surrender on the boxer's behalf.

Wilde was physically wrecked; his right eye was almost closed, his left cheek was gashed. He stood like a soldier without arms as he went foolishly, into battle as the seventh bell rang.

Professionals understand and admire a champion who prefers to go down like a champion, but there are also times when blind bravery should not be allowed. The crowd yelled 'Stop it' as Wilde stumbled forward and the referee glanced at Villa as though asking the executioner to quickly finish his job. Villa cocked his powerful right and cracked a short hook that landed flush on Wilde's chin. For a second Wilde remained motionless, then he half-turned and fell flat on his face in a neutral corner. No count was necessary. The referee raised Pancho's arm, then quickly waved him away to allow Wilde's seconds to carry their man back to the corner.

The crowd rose as one to hail Wilde's courage. They reckoned he had looked better in defeat than many champions in victory.

The battered little Welshman went out with a touch of humility. 'I was beaten on the night by a better man,' he said, 'Pancho is a great champion.'

For Wilde, like many a champion, it was a question of having one fight too many.

He returned to the Welsh valleys and lived in a big, old red house called Ael-y-Bryn at Cadoxton. He owned a cinema at Barry and for many years put his name to a boxing column in the Sunday *News of the World*. He frequently described the ringmen of the sixties as 'bloody slow'.

Despite the car crash and the indignity of being butted in the face by a teenage thug, Wilde did not indulge in any of the self-pitying bravado that disfigures many champions in eclipse. But he did permit himself to become grossly overweight. He once weighed ten stone.

Index

Index